Called Together

Ngozi Martin-Oguike

BookMarkers • Nigeria

First published in 1998

ISBN: 9789788088530

Published in Nigeria by

BookMarkers Nigeria
93 Ashi/Bashorun Road, Bodija Ibadan.
&
No.5 Bukar Shuaibu Road, ABU Qrtrs C, Samaru Zaria.

Email: onagwa@gmail.com
Phone: 234-805-513-9010, 234-813-300-6067

DEDICATION

To
Harold and Cordelia Oguike,
who together served the Lord in His vineyard.

Table of Contents

ACKNOWLEDGEMENTS

I wish to appreciate the valuable help rendered to me by some close friends and associates in bringing this book to its present form.

My thanks go to His Grace, the Most Rev. Dr. B. C. Nwankiti and his wife, Mrs. Jane J. Nwankiti and His Lordship, the Rt. Rev. U.U. Ezuoke and his wife, Mrs. S.C. Ezuoke, who have continued to encourage us in the ministry.

I want to give thanks to Rev. Clement U. Kelechukwu and Brother Emma Ndukwe for their patience in reading this manuscript and words of encouragement. Thanks also to all clergy and wives of St. Stephen's Pro-Cathedral and Trinity Theological College, Umuahia, with whom I have served for several years, gaining from their interaction.

Many thanks to the management and staff of Government Press, Umuahia, for their cooperation as individuals and their contribution to the production of this piece. My gratitude also goes to my parents, Mr. and Mrs. N.A.C. Opara, whose contributions to my upbringing, work and experience are invaluable. My husband, the Venerable Dr Martin Oguike, insisted that I should publish this book. Without his interest and push, I guess this would have ended up as wishful thinking. Thank God that his encouragement has come to reality.

I also want to acknowledge the contributions of Dr Felicia Ibezim, who proofread and edited the original manuscript, also, thanks to my daughter, Precious Emelumba, who retyped the original book and made valuable suggestions for improvement. I must appreciate my brother-inlaw and my sister, Dr Obed and Dr Mrs. Chizoma Ndikom of the Federal University of Technology, Owerri and University of Ibabdan respectively, for their support and encouragement and for being my publishing agents in Nigeria.

Thanks to all readers of the 1998 publication, especially those who encouraged me to republish it.

I am also grateful to all our great fathers and mothers in the faith, from whom I have learnt lots of lessons of life. Above all, Praise the Lord! If it had not been for the Lord, life itself would have been purposeless, so in the words of the psalmist, therefore, I acknowledge the God of blissful marriage, in Jesus' name. Amen.

I will give thanks to the Lord with my whole heart. In the company of the upright, in the congregation. Great are the works of the Lord, studied by all who have pleasure in them. Full honour and majesty is His work and His righteousness endures forever. Psa 111: 1 – 3.

FOREWORD

Many scholars and clerics down the centuries have spilled much erudite ink on the subject of the work and office of a pastor. But much has not been done in the area of the pastor's wife who is equally called alongside the husband.

Mrs. Ngozi Martin-Oguike, with her experience and involvement as wife of a pastor, provides us with this beautiful piece, titled *Called Together*. This great literary piece deals with the work and office of the pastor's wife within the context of her husband's ministry. Ngozi's experience as a Travelling Secretary with the Nigeria Fellowship of Evangelical Students (NIFES) exposed her a great deal to work among youths. Also, for many years, she has been involved in the training of ordinand's wives, as well as young pastors' wives.

In handling this subject, the author deals with many theological and pastoral issues, such as the call to service, the ministry of the church, engagement and marriage, life as a pastor's wife, Christian family life, and so on. She starts with a definition of 'calling', with such examples as Noah, Abraham, Moses, Joshua and Paul and goes on to deal with God's call to all to receive salvation.

Much is said here about God's call into the ordained ministry as touching a pastor, as well as his wife. For those women who are already married to ordained pastors, she reminds them that their marriage vow to live together with their husbands in obedience and service all the days of their lives implies acceptance of the ordained ministry as equally their own calling. This book gives a proper guidance as to how to lay a good foundation for Christian marriage and how to nurture it. There is much in the book to help Christian couples and especially those in the ordained ministry, which will enable them to have fruitful ministry, as well as a successful marriage.

Ngozi Martin-Oguike has had a long desire to write a book that will encourage pastors' wives of all Christian denominations to understand their role in the whole ministry of the Church. It is a book that could assist any pastor or Christian man or woman to see his or her ministry in perspective. She has indeed demonstrated much Christian scholarship.

I specially commend and recommend this book to all pastors and pastors' wives. It is highly recommended for theological students and pastors who need to understand that their wives are equally called with them. This book is very much needed today when pastors' wives are increasingly feeling that it is the pastors alone who have been called. *Called Together* will definitely open the eyes of such wives to understand that we are called together. All serious Christians, young and old, male and female will have a lot to learn to enrich their Christian lives and stabilize their marriages. The literary style which she employed in this book is unique and makes for pleasant reading. The book can become a good resource material for researchers in the same or similar subjects.

Ngozi Martin-Oguike has herself been a very faithful and committed pastor's wife and a virtuous Christian lady; hence, this book is not a mere precept but a book filled with practical examples. My prayer is that the book will become a blessing to many Christian homes.

Rev. Canon Martin Oguike
1998.

PREFACE

The aim of marriage is to strengthen and not destroy mankind. As such, if one fails to trust the Lord and depend on Him, matrimony becomes a nightmare. With my sincere desire to know the will of God for marriage as an institution of its own, I opened my heart to the Almighty God and He ministered to me and continues to educate me on the deep Christian principles concerning family life and the ministry of Christian couples. At some point, it became so overwhelming that I was moved to put them down into writing. This gave birth to *Called Together*.

The message has been embellished with lots of real-life stories, which are meant to drive the message home to the reader. The family should be a place of joy and happiness. The success of a couple in the ministry depends on the stability of the family and the extent of cordial relationship between a man and his wife (I Tim. 3: 4, 5). The Christian home is "a city set on the hilltop which cannot be hidden" (Matt. 5:14).

Called Together is a call to soberness, diligence, commitment and spiritual liberty, which make marriage wholesome and bring man closer to God's kingdom. Its message dispels all kinds of fears and explains the purpose of marital unity. It touches basic aspects of personal relationship and points us to other people's mistakes so we can avoid them.

After twenty years of first publishing *Called Together*, the message continues to enrich our family life and ministry. This message came as instruction from the throne of grace and has served as reference point for me so far in married life. It is a great pleasure to introduce this revised edition. It is the updated version for all Christian couples who desire to remain faithful partners in the gospel of Christ. Yes, we are called together to live in harmony and obedience to the heavenly calling.

In these days when iniquity abounds, here is a reminder to return to the basics of our faith and the purpose of marriage. This message is for both men and women who want to live for and serve the Lord. The Lord says, "Come unto me all that labor and are heavy laden and I will give you rest" Matthew 11:28. And after twenty seven years of married life, I am even more assured that *marriage is good, iron sharpenth iron, two is better than one, and a threefold cord is not easily broken. So the Lord made Adam, a help suitable for him.*

The real Christian home is the place of safety, peace and joy; therefore, I am presenting to you another resource that will help you rediscover God's purpose for Christian marriage. It is a book for couples who desire a keepsake for their walk with one another in the presence of our Almighty God. This is the original "Called Together" with additional thoughts and some new appendices. My prayer is that we all shall be strong until the day of His coming.

I earnestly pray that youths, newlyweds, married couples, men and women, as well as elders and pastors will find *Called Together* a worthy counsellor.

Ngozi Martin-Oguike.

Bone of My Bone

"It is not good," says the Lord,
"For the man to stay alone."
For the emptiness in Him yearns to be filled,
The race is run in companionship,
For one helps the other when he falls.
Yet walking together needs a perfect pair.
For bone must click with its own bone,
And flesh cannot fit into strange flesh.
Adam must be Eve's husband,
For satisfaction at the dawn of the day.

Ngozi Martin-Oguike

Chapter 1

CALL TO SERVICE

alling is a term used in reformation theology for the act of persuading people to receive salvation through accepting the good news of our Lord Jesus Christ[1]. To call means to summon, or cry out to someone for a purpose. The Lord has given man a will to choose good instead of evil. He beckons on people to come into His vineyard and allows them to choose whether or not to accept Him. There is a general call to all (see John 3:16) and there is a specific call into different vocations in God's service.

Joshua beckoned on the Israelites, saying 'Choose you this day whom you will serve' (Joshua 24:15a). It is a call to choose, to decide either to serve the Lord or to serve other gods. It was a day of salvation. In like manner, the Lord called Noah to be a preacher of righteousness in his generation and asked him to build an ark for the saving of his household. Noah obeyed and was saved. He also called Abraham to go to the Promised Land and assured him of blessings and prosperity. Abraham obeyed and received God's blessings.

Saul was called on his way to Damascus. The Lord declared that He would use him and show him how much he must suffer for the gospel (Acts 9). Paul was an apostle called to go to the Gentiles, while Peter worked among his Jewish brethren. All these men performed their duties and the Lord recognized them and blessed them mightily. Each one was commended for his faithfulness in a calling. In each case, however, it was a specific call to a known mission. The Lord calls and equips each one for the task ahead.

Furthermore, Moses was called through the burning bush. Prior to that experience, he was trained in Pharaoh's palace as a prince of Egypt; little did he know that it was in preparation for him to deliver the people of Israel from Egyptian bondage. He went into the land of Midian where he became a shepherd and this was an indirect way of training him to be a pastor of God's people, leading them to Canaan.

The Lord accomplishes His purpose in our lives through every circumstance we pass through. At a stage in one's life, God's call to a specific purpose becomes vivid. Prior to this, the Christian feels unsettled and unaccomplished until he begins to serve God in this area, thus receiving peace and fulfilment in service. A sincere and prayerful child of God who is faithful in service will hear clearly from the Father.

Some children of God may decide to work where they are not called. When this happens, there is confusion in the ministry. To be in God's will requires praying and asking God for leading and obeying Him when He speaks to you. The general calling to all is to receive salvation: 'Behold I stand at the door and knock, if anyone hears my voice and opens the door I will come in to him' (Rev. 3: 20). This is for everyone, because the Lord Jesus says: 'Whosoever believes in Him will not perish but have everlasting life' (John 3:16b). It is not the will of the Father that any of us should perish; hence, He sends His ministers everywhere to preach the good news of salvation. He commissions believers with the message of reconciliation, reconciling us to God and to one another. This call is to people of all nations, all tribes, all languages and all kindred (Rev. 7:9). Every one of this group will be represented at the final gathering of the people of God. Therefore, God calls men and women to function in all areas of human endeavours as ambassadors of Christ; some as pastors, teachers, doctors, lawyers, engineers, nurses, traders, pilots, sailors, farmers, and so on. Therefore, no one has any excuse on the last day: 'Wherefore, seeing we also are compassed about with so great a cloud of witnesses, let us lay aside every weight and sin that doth so easily beset us' (Heb. 12:1).

There is no calling that is of greater importance than the other. The key is to be faithful in our place of calling no matter how despised it may look. The Bible makes a special reference to those who are teachers among us. That would include pastors, teachers, evangelists, prophets and apostles. If you hold these offices in the church or you are a secular teacher, you must be very careful. 'Thou therefore which teacheth another teacheth thou not thyself? Thou that preacheth a man should not steal, dost thou steal?' (Rom. 2:21).

For those who have answered to God's calling into full-time or ordained ministry, they should be sure that the Lord has indeed called them in a vivid way. They must be faithful shepherds of God's flock, not leading the flock astray. They must be faithful stewards who will be accountable to their Master.

Calling is an individual affair, so God deals with each one as an individual. When the Lord wants to deal with a couple, He will do it in such a way that they will both be persuaded of the Lord's calling. If a young woman is getting married to someone who is already a pastor or a full-time minister, she should share in his vision. These two are called together into the ministry. The day of marriage is the beginning of this covenant relationship that incorporates all areas of their lives, especially God's calling.

As the wife makes her marriage vow to live together with the husband, she indirectly accepts his area of calling and agrees to be obedient, serving him all the days of their lives. Therefore, she is called alongside him. This is an issue she should have taken out time to think and pray about, and receive advice on. This is in accordance with the marriage charge, which often reads in part as:

> And therefore is not by any to be enterprised nor taken in hand, unadvisedly, lightly or wantonly, to satisfy men's carnal lusts and appetites, like brute beasts, that have no understanding, but reverently, discreetly, advisedly, soberly and in the fear of God; duly considering the causes for which matrimony was ordained...[2]

This is the right step to take before a woman gets into this divine institution of marriage, because she cannot exonerate herself from her husband's calling, for the Lord who joins them together intends that they should be united in all things.

For the sake of order in God's government, the Lord intends the man to be the head of the woman (1Corinthians 11:3). The man must be the husband of the woman. She could have her own area of service and enjoy it until she gets to know a man who shares her calling. As soon as they are married, they should walk together to accomplish the task ahead. The man is the head of the family and should be recognized as such. He should also be responsible enough to prove his headship.

In humility, he should give his wife respect and honour. He should discover her gifts and encourage her to develop them. If they work together and are spiritual, they will always remain an entity. A couple should always remember the day they were declared one. The Anglicans have a beautiful symbolic mode of sealing the marriage covenant. The officiating priest ties the bride's and groom's hands together with a stole (a cloth strap worn on the neck over the surplice). He prays for them and declares: 'What God has joined together, let no man put asunder.' This is known as tying the nuptial knot. Every remembrance of this should cause a couple to remain one.

Chapter 2

A PURE FOUNDATION

But as He which hath called you is holy, so be ye holy in all manner of conversation. I Peter1: 15

As it is in every other institution of God, marriage should be approached in holiness and awe. This is because we serve a holy and righteous God. Two persons do not just see each other for the first time and decide to marry. Marriage is much deeper than that. Just as in our individual calling, God is the one who institutes marriage and, for that reason, He purifies and executes it.

When a young man is ready to marry, no one can stop him from looking for a suitable young lady. As he prays, he also looks out until he finds the person he desires. He is convinced that this person is the one he loves so dearly and desires to be with all the time. If that is the case, how should they comport themselves before marriage? Couples have to go through a relatively brief period of closeness prior to marriage. This is called courtship. The period of courtship is a time of knowing each other and deciding to work together in several areas of life. This is, above all, a time of praying for the future as husband and wife.

For a reasonable couple, this should be approached with prayerfulness and openness. First of all, the couple should boldly introduce each other to their parents and relatives so that whatever they are doing will not be hidden. Their pastors should also be kept abreast of the relationship, so as to give the right kind of guidance that is needed as they proceed. If there is courtship without a focus, it might become an endless relationship that might not result in marriage.

Bimpe was a student in one of our universities and had a relationship with a Christian young man for two years. Tunde had a broken relationship before he got to know Bimpe and they related very fine. Their friendship was known all over the campus with a general assumption that they were courting; yet Bimpe was not settled with that. She came to me one day and our discussion went this way:

'Sister, I guess you think I am engaged?' she queried,

'Yes, I suppose so' I answered. 'Am I wrong?'

'That is actually why I am here. I came to ask you what the real meaning of engagement is. I am not sure of my relationship with Tunde.' She confessed.

'Well, Bimpe, tell me what you are really going through and I will be in a position to advise you.'

Bimpe began to tell me her story. She had discovered that Tunde was having problems that hindered him from socializing on campus. One day, she visited him to discuss the matter. Tunde was happy and relieved to tell the story of his past experience. His ex-fiancée had jilted him and got married to a close friend of theirs. He felt so shattered and betrayed. His self-esteem was crushed and he could no longer trust friends, whether male or female.

With great compassion, Bimpe shared scriptures with him and prayed, exhorting him with Philippians 3:10-11. He was extremely impressed and felt that she was the only person in the world that cared about him in his situation. This resulted in a sincere love for Bimpe. There developed a companionship that became so obvious that people began to raise eyebrows. They walked, prayed and read together on campus. After two years, Tunde did not propose to her. Bimpe was so concerned and did not know how to end the relationship. She did not want to hurt him, but she desired to be free.

I sympathized with Bimpe. As far as I am concerned, she was not engaged. She was in an undefined relationship for two years and needed to disengage from it for her own sake. The foundation was really faulty.

An engagement is a formal arrangement. It involves two persons who have agreed to get married and have involved their families in their plans. In most Nigerian cultures, the parents of the young man take wine to the lady's parents and they all approve of their children's plans. Then, an engagement is started. But it is not yet time for the girl to go and live with her suitor. This is not culturally accepted and is unchristian. Any affair or cohabitation at this time is regarded as extramarital and is fornication because they are not yet married. It is a time to draw up a schedule that will lead to wedding ceremonies, culminating in holy wedlock, as recognized by the church and society.

This should be a time to express their minds to each other, pray together for the future and get close Christian friends to pray for them. Sincerity in sharing with one another should be their preoccupation. Simple conversations can be eye-openers as they discuss their desires for the future in terms of ambitions, aspirations, visions and ministry interests. It is a time to read between the lines as one cannot work with a spouse whose ambitions and interests are in conflict.

Eventually, Bimpe admitted to me that she liked Tunde but could not marry him because he was an aimless Christian. He possessed no distinct spiritual gifts but was more interested in making money than in seeking the kingdom of God. She, like most Christian girls, wanted to marry a man who would serve the Lord devotedly to the end. The two broke up and separated in good faith after a series of joint counselling sessions. Bimpe is now married to a sound Christian minister.

While planning marriage, a couple will certainly get to know each other closely. It is good to be sincere to one another. Do not be too high-handed. Let your spouse know what you have and plan within your means. The society is full of showmanship. Christians should not be like the world. We should be different. If a husband or wife is going to be a spendthrift, this is the time to find out. Let Christian ethics guide in all plans and preparations. This is the time to decide fully or change your mind on whether to get married or not. If there is any reason not to go into matrimony, it is right to say it. It is better to go into it without bias. Cultural, health and spiritual issues must be settled. Each person must be fully persuaded. As the priest would read out at the solemnization of holy matrimony:

> I require and charge you both, as ye will answer at the dreadful Day of Judgment when the secrets of all

hearts shall be disclosed, that if either of you know any impediment, why you may not be lawfully joined together in matrimony, ye do now confess it, for be ye well assured that as many as are coupled together otherwise than God's Word doth allow are not joined together by God, neither is their matrimony lawful.[3]

For these reasons, inhibitions should be confessed before this day so that you can stand before God and declare that all is well. Certain people have got married only to hear later that their husbands had children by other women or vice versa. Others have heard that their spouses have other spouses in faraway countries. Often, these situations lead to divorce or other problems. Therefore, every past issue should be confessed, including underlying sicknesses, past relationships, etc. These days of medical advancements, it will be proper to discuss genotype, blood group, Rhesus factor and age. The knowledge of these should not affect true love, but should enable one to get into marriage fully aware of its challenges.

Family backgrounds should be discussed and prayers said for members of each family regularly right from the beginning. The couple should be fully committed to one another. Do not allow your eyes to be coveting another man or woman's spouse. One's ability to keep to his wife or husband contributes principally to the success of a marriage. This is known as faithfulness and it is the bedrock of marital stability and joy.

After the ceremonies of wedding, there is still work to be done. The couple must avoid all forms of impurity and negligence of one another, remembering the marriage vows and the consequences of disobedience: 'Forsaking all others, keep thee only unto her/him as long as you both shall live.'[4] As long as the two have agreed to get married, the commitment should continue in the mind and body, just as the word of God commands: 'Flee all youthful lust, follow righteousness, faith, charity, peace with them that call on the Lord out of a pure heart' (II Timothy 2:22).

Chapter 3

DENY YOURSELF

If any man will come after me, Let him deny himself, take up his cross and follow me. Matthew 16:24

Mgbechi was an enterprising young lady, who was very enlightened and loved by her family. She was a disciplined young woman from the east who wanted to make heaven. She started to get suitors long before she was ready for marriage. Eventually, she got close to a man from one of the northern states who proposed to her. Bala was a very committed Christian who was training to be a pastor. He had a vivid call into the ministry. How could she accept this double responsibility of intercultural marriage and call to ministry? 'The spirit is willing but the flesh is weak' (Matthew 26: 41b). Mgbechi did not understand how to go about this situation because she was convinced that Bala was the right man for her. She let him stay in the dark for a while, as she neither accepted nor rejected his proposal, but really loved him. It appeared real and not based on emotion. Yet, she was unsure how to proceed.

When Mgbechi eventually came for counselling, she was terribly confused. Tearfully she stated, 'Auntie, to be sincere with you, I want to get married to Bala, but I wish he was neither from the north nor a minister. I know my parents would object.' And she was right. Her family did not accept the relationship. The counsellor had advised her to go on and accept the proposal so long as she loved him. She was advised to divorce her mind from tribal sentiments and, rather, pray for God's direction on what to do. After two years, she accepted the proposal. Bala was still patiently waiting. However, when they went to see Mgbechi's parents, the main battle began. They blatantly rejected their intention, warning Bala to stay away from their beloved daughter. This led to eight long years of waiting, at the end of which they finally got married in a glorious wedding extravaganza. Of course, Mgbechi's parents also graced the occasion and were exceedingly glad. The couple had passed through lots of trials in which the Lord granted them strength, peace and fulfilment.

Mgbechi met me recently and shared the testimony of what the Lord did in her life. 'I am glad I learnt a lot of lessons through my experience,' she said, recounting marvellous breakthroughs that the Lord had given to them. First of all, she learnt to pray through during those years. Her love for Bala caused her not to falter or change her mind for any other man. She prayed ceaselessly and fervently for her parents until the Lord changed their minds and turned their resentment into acceptance for him, as a son. Also, she learnt to commit her endeavours into the hands of God. This God Who has so marvellously endowed her with beauty, talents and knowledge wanted to use her in a predominantly Muslim land as a pastor's wife. Why not resign to His will?

Moreover, she began to understand what the Lord meant by 'take up your cross and follow me'. Yes, to stand her ground meant to bear a cross. During those eight years of waiting, many affluent and influential suitors proposed to her, but they looked vain in her eyes. The Lord certainly prepared her for the work of the ministry. Within that period also, she learnt to lead different Christian groups: girls, children, youth, Bible study classes, prayer groups, and so on. In fact, it was a delay that was pre-planned and executed by the Lord, and when all the lessons were learnt, there came a wonderful breakthrough. This gorgeous lady learnt her lesson and today, she is occupying a position as a mother and a friend of the needy, meeting numerous needs and solving their problems. Mgbechi learnt faithfulness, which is the basis of successful marriage and ministry.

In Christian marriage, there is daily self-denial. A friend of ours describes marriage as the beginning of the cure for selfishness. For one to decide to get married, he or she must be ready to love enough to give up fully what belongs to self.

> Wives, submit yourselves unto your own husbands as unto the Lord… Therefore, as the church is subject unto Christ, so let the wives be to their own husbands in everything. *Ephesians 5:22, 24*

In these times when most girls marry relatively late due to prevailing circumstances, a good number of new wives are set in their ways. They are used to their methods and find it hard to fit into any other system. Little wonder why many cannot submit to their husbands in their homes, as submission seems to be an outdated virtue. Yet, part of the Lord's teaching on self-denial is that wives should submit themselves to their own husbands as to the Lord in everything. This may be hard, but the reason why two righteous hearts should be knit together in marriage is that they help one another to keep to holy and righteous living. It is easier for a Christian woman to be submissive to a godly husband than to an ungodly man. The sure way to have a chaotic family is for a Christian to marry a non-Christian partner. It becomes more difficult to deny yourself. All the same, the word of God does not change. The rule remains, 'Likewise ye wives be in subjection to your own husbands, that if any obey not the word, they also may, without the word, be won by the conversation of the wives" (I Peter 3:1).

For those whose husbands do not obey the word, they must be submissive for another reason; that they can show a good example to their husbands so that they will repent. A wife who is fully devoted wins her husband to the Lord. A family with mutual submission and love receives answers to their prayers.

Starting a new marital home, one is made to open up to many more relatives and friends. It is easier to remain bottled up and unfriendly to your spouse's friends and relations. But part of self-denial is that even when those friends and family members are not the type you cherish, you have to accept them because of the unity of marriage. Do not scare them away.

As much as possible, a wife's dressing should reflect her husband's taste. On getting married, I was often offended when my husband disapproved of my dressing. I felt he was difficult to please, but I soon discovered that it was not all the time that his own outfits pleased me. With time, we understood ourselves much better. This is an area of self-denial. In the past, I could go off even without seeing how I looked, since it appeared that no one was looking at me. But this is no longer the case. A woman does things to please her husband (1Corinthians 7:4, 33).

Uduak got married last Christmas and travelled with her husband on honeymoon. They spent two weeks in Jos and had a time of real refreshing. Uduak was still full of plans for her job. She was involved with a company that expected her to return to work immediately, but Etim, her husband, had ordered that she should stop work forthwith. She must resign as soon as they returned home. It was difficult for her to understand why. For Etim, she did not need to do such a tedious job and so ought to resign and take up a less intensive job nearer home.

There was a major dispute between the couple. In fact, that was their first argument ever since they met each other. Uduak was intent on continuing her enviable career, but Etim, in a resolute manner, said 'No' and that was it. Uduak resigned and now stays home without a job. Whether it was a good decision or not, what is important is that she submitted to her husband instead of tearing the young family apart. The best approach would have been to discuss this plan before marriage, but Etim, like many men, became emboldened after their wedding and asserted himself.

Yet, a godly woman is not intent on having her way. She allows her husband to be her head. As it were, she 'aids her husband's honour'. The virtuous or ideal woman keeps the confidence of her husband (Proverbs 31:11) and seeks what is good for him (v. 10). Furthermore, this woman aids in the prosperity and honour of her husband. 'Her husband is known in the gates, when he sitteth among the elders of the land' (Proverbs 31:23). Sitting at the city gate in ancient times indicated that the man held a position of honour and leadership. Lot, for example, sat at the gates of Sodom (Genesis 19:1).

"The husband of a virtuous woman is found sitting in the gates among the leaders in a godly community to help judge the people. That was the place of the courts. The virtuous woman is concerned that her husband had an honourable position."[5] A woman should help project her husband and bring honour to him. It is not her place to bring him down (Proverbs 31: 23). A husband should respect and love his wife. None of them should bring shame to the family. It calls for self-denial and obedience to God's Word.

Chapter 4

THE LAW OR THE SPIRIT OF MARRIAGE?

The Pharisees were a legalistic group of people who chose the option of any available loophole in the law. They could not allow themselves to seek the deeper things of the spirit. They were very religious. That was why they went to Jesus to ask Him a question concerning marriage; whether it was unlawful for a man to put away his wife for 'every course'. Jesus answered that it was not good because God, in the beginning, made them male and female. 'Wherefore, they are no twain, but one flesh. What therefore God hath joined together, let no man put asunder' (Matthew 19:6). The Pharisees, in their argumentative style, asked Him why Moses commanded that they could give a 'writing of divorcement' (that is, a letter of divorce) and therefore separate. Jesus' answer is very poignant: 'Moses because of the hardness of your hearts suffered you to put away your wives; but from the beginning it was not so' (Matthew 19:8).

It is not God's intention for us to divorce nor is it the best method of resolving a marital issue. When two people are married under God, they become one flesh and should remain so till death parts them. Any reason for divorce should be avoided because it is against the will of God. The Pharisees taught divorce, but Jesus taught reconciliation. If the two are divorced, the issue of divorce becomes very controversial, following Jesus' teaching in Matthew 19:9 – 10: 'Whosoever shall put away his wife, except it be for fornication and shall marry another committeth adultery and whoso marrieth her which is put away doth commit adultery.'

It is notable that God permitted divorce for just one reason, adultery or fornication. For a wife or husband to be with another person, it means that she or he has defiled the marriage bed; that she or he has despised and broken the marriage vows. Yet, forgiveness could bring about reconciliation. But due to the hardness of man's heart, Jesus put a condition: if they remarry, then they would be living in adultery. This may be hard to deal with, but this is the word of God for us. Christian marriage is one man, one woman, whole and indivisible.

Since the teaching of the Lord is of love, and love covers a multitude of sins (I Peter 4:8), then there is no sin that cannot be forgiven and forgotten for the sake of peace and harmony in this holy institution of marriage. The reason behind a person's decision to get married is very important, as it helps him or her to get prepared for the uncertainties that are ahead. Some want to marry because they feel that their age mates are married; some, because they want to settle down and have children; others, because they have fallen in love. These are all good reasons. None is a sinful reason, but one should be ready to face the challenges of marriage, holding unto the Lord who instituted marriage for the sanctity of human life. It is right to have an unselfish reason for whatever we do. God should be the centre of our desire in marriage. It is easy for a man to take his wife for granted if he were unprepared for marriage. He can also disrespect his wife if there was no love for her. Such a couple would likely not be able to work together. This is a sure way to failure in marriage. Marriage should be embarked upon out of a full conviction of God's leading.

Marriage is a contract and the marriage vows are binding, not only here on earth but also in heaven; 'Again I say to you, That if two of you shall agree on earth as touching anything that they shall ask, it shall be done for them of my Father in heaven' (Matthew 18:19). Marriage is a physical arrangement that is signed by God Himself. The fact that it can be dissolved here on earth does not mean that heaven allows it. That is why those who desire to marry should take time to pray and wait on the Lord for direction before they embark upon marriage. Once vows have been exchanged, the biblical injunction is that no one breaks them. The couple could step on each other's toes, but if they believe in each other's good intentions they will easily forgive and march on to victory. Family prayers are key to keeping the family spiritually alert, for 'the family that prays together stays together'.

Some marriage relationships have weakened to the extent that each partner is looking for fault and excuses for separation or unfaithfulness. However, Jesus has given us the Spirit of reconciliation and has prayed that we all may be one. Therefore, it will be a shame if any of us tries to tear apart what God has established. A marriage that is just a legal contract and without the will of God is that which lacks love, joy, peace and safety. A troubled family affects us, as Jacqueline's experience reveals. I met her as an undergraduate.

Most of Jacqueline's mates discussed their wishes for the future; a safe home, a faithful husband, and lovely children, but not so with Jackey. She wanted to remain single, study hard and get a PhD, then live in Lagos and travel out of the country from time to time. She would have liked to have children but as a Christian she would resort to child adoption. Jackey had just one reason for her decision, her parents had been separated since she was five. Even though she was now a Christian and knew better, she still could not trust a man and so kept turning down proposals. I do hope she gets happily married someday.

Jackey's parents were legally divorced; they also both got remarried—this is not always the case, however. What about many parents who are living together in the same house without actually being united? Some say the wife is not submissive, others, the husband is unfaithful, or they made a mistake. All these will not do. It often leads to psychological problems for the children, who grow up not knowing what love is. Is there any sacrifice too much for us to make in order to bring up our young ones in all aspects of life? It is frightening to have to make a choice between Mom and Dad. Christians should never create that problem for their children. Marriage should never be looked at just as the signing of a legal document, because lives are involved and would be altered with if this 'document' is torn or trashed. It is rather a spiritual issue that affects emotions. The society values marriage and God established and seals it.

Chapter 5

THE FAMILY WITH OR WITHOUT CHILDREN

A home is a dwelling place, a fixed residence of a family or household. A nuclear family is made up of the father, mother and children. Other helpers and relatives can be part of the family from time to time. This is called the extended family, as is still practised in Africa, and it includes the grandparents, uncles, aunts, nieces, nephews and cousins. These extended family members all live in the home. The Christian household is, on the other hand, a home for all believers. It is also a place of fellowship with other Christians. It is a place of love and care for one another. Despite this extension, the family must be a place of real affinity between its members, because it is a unit of the church. If our churches are made up of happy families, then the church will be a happy one.

A family is formed on the day a man and a woman are wedded in the presence of some witnesses. The efforts of the husband and wife are needed in order to keep the family united. One of the prayers said for a couple at the wedding service is that they may bear children. This is often looked upon as the ultimate result of marriage. It is the desire of most couples to bear children and have their own offspring, but where this is delayed or not forthcoming, what should the Christian attitude be?

The Bible commands as well as promises us fruitfulness with regards to the fruit of the womb. But not all marriages result in the birth of children. Some choose not to have children, others may have a problem that delays childbearing or may, for one medical reason or the other, not be able to procreate. However, the couple must work together to seek a solution to the problem. Issues like that should not result in blaming each other, rather a couple should go for medical investigation. Causes of infertility has shown that about 25% of causes are from the woman and 25% from the man, while the remaining 50% are caused by factors that have to do with both male and female. (Llwellyn-Jone, 1986). Proper diagnoses as well as solutions must be sought. This happens to a great number of couples and is not the end of the world. It does not call for regrets or indifference to one another. Instead, the couple should seek the face of God, praying and fasting like Hannah until the Lord answers.

Testimonies abound of couples who have been healed of infertility by God, long after doctors have certified them barren or impotent. Obviously, the difficult time of waiting should be a period of occupying one's mind with so much more for the kingdom of God to reduce anxiety, as we are commanded: 'Be anxious for nothing, but in everything by prayer and supplication, with thanksgiving, let your requests be made known to God' (Philippians 4:6). This is because anxiety will not yield any positive fruit; hence, it is a time to take up the challenge of living for the Lord in the midst of the problem.

The most likely event after a wedding is for the new wife to become pregnant in a couple of months. During this period, the mother-to-be is carrying the conceived foetus in her womb. It is the time of care and adjustment for the family. The woman would just discover that her regular monthly periods have ceased; in some cases, she could suffer from nausea and vomiting, may urinate frequently, and would definitely have a bulging stomach as the baby grows. Some women suffer from body aches, general discomfort, itching of the skin, and many other symptoms.

> Men react to their wives' pregnancies with various feelings: protectiveness of the wife, increased pride in the marriage, pride about their virility (that is one thing men always worry about to some degree), and anticipatory enjoyment of the child. But there can also be way underneath, a feeling of being left out (just as small children may feel rejected when they find that their mother is pregnant) which can be expressed as grumpiness towards his wife, wanting to spend more evenings with his men friends or flirtatiousness with other women. These reactions are no help to the wife who craves extra support at the start of this unfamiliar stage of her life (Spock, 1998).

When negative reactions ensue, the marriage relationship passes through so much stress that the relationship is threatened if the man cannot keep the vow of 'for better, for worse, in sickness and in health' (The Book of Common Prayer). When the mother-to-be begins to attend regular antenatal check-ups as pregnancy is confirmed, it is the duty of the husband to see that she is taken proper care of; that she has the right diet, rests adequately and has money to cover her requirements. Some fathers-to-be do not see these as their duties. The woman suffers alone through forty or more weeks. Since there are two people in the family who have agreed to bear children together, the two should share in the process of the new arrival into their home. The husband needs to ensure that the baby's needs are purchased and that the wife is ready before the expected date of delivery. This is a source of encouragement to the pregnant mother.

In some hospitals and maternities, the authorities at the labour wards would require the husband to stay by his wife at the moment of labour and delivery. By so doing, he participates and learns from the experience as he welcomes the new miracle of God. In some other places, the husband may indicate his desire to accompany his wife to the labour room and they may or may not allow him. It is important that all husbands stay by their wives through the delivery process. It helps them to appreciate more in the miracle of God's creation. Each time I had a baby, my husband was right there. He has been a great source of encouragement; praying for me and sharing in my pain. It is a very effective way of having our babies together. Those experiences have not left us as we bring up our children. I think oneness should get to that extent and more.

After pregnancy, and soon after delivery, the mother experiences weakness of the body, which affects her looks. The new mother may not look as pretty as she used to be; she may pay more attention to her new baby than to her husband. The husband should realize and be encouraged by the fact that it is just for a short time. Soon, if he is patient and caring, their relationship would be better than ever before as the stressful period does not last forever. As such, the man should not shy away from being part of the child's upbringing. Both parents should bring the baby close to them for the bonding that occurs as a result of close contact with the baby. Ideally, this begins immediately after birth, as both parents and baby benefit from this relationship and love that flourish through bonding. Any of the parents who feels that he or she should not be bothered about closeness with the infant should not complain when the child would later prefer the company of the one that was present during his or her upbringing.

The plan for child spacing and desired number of children to have, as well as the methods to use should be agreed upon and handled maturely. This is otherwise known as family planning. It should be prayerfully embarked upon. The care of the family should be a joint effort. House work should be done in the spirit of equal partnership. 'The benefit is lost if the work is done as a favour to the wives, since this implies that it is not really the husband's job but just an unusual degree of generosity on his part" (Spock, 1998). The children will also benefit from experiencing a variety of styles of leadership and control. The father collaborates with the mother to run the family.

Invariably, parents should evolve a method of caring for the family spiritually. They should keep the family together in prayer, worship and sharing the Word of God. The children should be raised to know the Lord from the beginning (Proverbs 22:6). Family altar should be a regular feature of the Christian home. Young children should be regular in Sunday school, children's service, Bible Club and other children organizations that will help them grow up spiritually. They should go to the best schools affordable to their parents. Regularly, either or both parents should supervise homework and projects. Permissiveness does not help our children at any stage of their lives. Parents must be firm and speak with one voice in all things pertaining to discipline. There should be no conflicting messages.

Family Altar

The family altar can be seen as the place of prayer and study of the word of God in the household. It is not a physical altar but a system, whereby prayer and worship are organized in the Christian home. It represents access to God and a place of refuge in his presence. The reasons for family altar in the home include:

1. Togetherness, Acts 2:1
2. Unity of purpose, Amos 3:3
3. Teaching the Word to the household, Prov. 22:6, Jos. 1:8
4. Involving the children in our spiritual growth, Jos. 4:6,7
5. Fellowship at the grassroots, Hebrews10:25
6. Bearing one another's burden, Galatians 6:1,2
7. A necessary time of prayer

How to hold a prayer session

    a. Gather the members of the family by calling them.

    b. One person should be in charge of conducting the prayer each day. Everybody in the home should be involved.

c. Pray, sing choruses or hymns, and study the Bible systematically. It is advisable to use a Daily Reading note such as *Daily Guide, Daily Power, Our Daily Bread, Family Altar* or you read sequentially from one book of the Bible to the other.

d. Ask questions, collect prayer points, give testimonies of answered prayers. Teach the children how to pray (Luke 11:1).

e. Share prayer points or needs.

f. Pray to close.

Adopt innovations that make your family prayers interesting. These are the family peculiarities. In my family for instance, every youngest baby has a favourite chorus. Songs are known as PP's chorus, Praise's chorus, Daddy's chorus, etc. Whenever we say, 'surely', everybody will hold hands together smiling as we confess the 'goodness of God'. If you begin the song, 'prayer is the key...' everyone automatically kneels down for prayers. If you are a visitor you will just follow. These are family traditions that bring joy, which stay with us even after years of leaving home.

For several reasons, there may be some variation in the time of prayer, but the key to a successful family altar is consistency. The hour of prayer should be adhered to, which could be morning, 5.00 am (Mark1:35), night time, before the youngest child goes to bed. Some days, the breakfast table could be the place of family altar. This is usually possible on Saturday mornings or on public holidays. It takes diligence to make this work.

Despite the fact that several pressing factors affect having a regular family altar, parents should make all efforts to ensure that they gather the entire family for daily family altar. Factors that can affect effective family altar are:

- Busy schedule
- Misunderstanding within the home
- Sin in the family
- Demonic influences
- Oversleeping and laziness
- Guests in the home
- Other extenuating factors, such as, personal quiet time, couple's prayer hour, morning prayer at the church or chapel, etc.

Nevertheless, the family should prayerfully keep the hour of prayer hallowed and organize the above factors out of their prayer time. In fact, sin, demonic influences, misunderstanding or such circumstances do hinder prayer. However, the hour of prayer should enable the family to keep such from lingering in the home. As the saying goes, 'if prayer does not keep you from sinning, sin will keep you from praying.' Do away with sin, confess and forsake it. Couples should not pretend to be super-spiritual to the outside world while their families suffer from spiritual draught. Busy schedules, even when they are for Christian programmes or morning chapel attendance, should never take the place of family altar. If morning is not working, then evening should be used. If there are clashes of activities, families should adjust their time and never take fellowship time for granted. The benefits of a successful family altar are numerous, and include:

- It makes for good interaction within the household.
- It is the main avenue for evangelism, nurturing and training of the child.
- During family altar all household problems could be handled in God's presence.
- It brings Christian discipline into family life.
- It instils the fear of God into our children and brings them to early repentance. Family altar saves them from many sorrows and brings a full man into God's service.
- Confidence in one another is cultivated through this fellowship.
- It is a socializing factor that helps the child to learn to read and lead, thereby removing stage fright from an early stage. (See more in Appendix E)

Family Finances

Any family that is not destroyed by financial crisis will remain a happy one. The apostle Paul said that 'the love of money is the root of all evil' (I Timothy 6:10). No family can exist without some monetary transactions. This is because the family is a unit or organization of its own. It is, therefore, ideal for family finances to be run centrally.

For most couples, it is rather unthinkable to run a joint account. This is due to several selfish reasons, as some think that having a joint account would limit their freedom to use their hard-earned money. Some forget the marriage vow: '...all my worldly goods with thee I share'. The best way to put it is that "there is love so long as there is no extra financial burden".

Audrey got engaged to Yomi with very lofty ideas about submissiveness and working together. Since Yomi was hers, she had to yield to him in everything. However, during courtship, Yomi began to educate her on the reasons why separate accounts will be good for them even though she seemed to know otherwise. He suggested that she should continue to run her personal account, while he has his own so that should there be any problem (either with a bank or an account) one account only suffer. He also felt that she could easily spend from her account without getting permission from him. It gave her some form of independence.

Audrey was not altogether pleased with his explanations, but she had to accept to make their marriage work. Yomi sounded crafty and self-seeking. After their wedding, Audrey secured a job, so her salaries were directly deposited into her account from time to time. Yomi also gave her allowance for upkeep. For as long as the going was good, the arrangement worked. Then Yomi lost his well-paid job. For more than a year, he stayed home without any income and he felt so bad, as his account became completely depleted so that he had to depend on Audrey for upkeep. It was more frustrating for him because he didn't know how much she earned and could not scrutinize her financial management. She prospered at her job and ran a little business that augmented their resources. This situation caused a lot of tension and humbled the egocentric Yomi. After this experience, he got a new job; he thereafter followed wise counsel and resolved to now run joint accounts.

Ada was another woman who felt that running a joint account was no good. Her husband believed that as Christians they ought to be one in everything, especially in the area of finance, even though he is the chief accountant of the family. Nevertheless, being a pretender to the core, Ada agreed to his terms but secretly opened a personal account, which was only known to her and a friend of hers. With time, their friendship deteriorated so that this so-called friend revealed the secret to her husband, causing a big crisis in their relationship which shook the foundation of trust in their marriage. They are yet to recover from that event. If a spouse runs any other account, it should be laid bare before the two.

The chronicle of families, both Christian and non-Christian homes, which have had crisis due to separate financial transactions is endless. For example, Isaac, an Alabama State Department of Education Supervisor, reported that he and his wife had disagreed over how their money was to be spent particularly on their children. But just as they shared household chores, they also had a joint account: *We have some friends who got separate accounts and gradually got a divorce,* he said (Ebony Magazine, June 1990). These were not Christians, but they understood the essence of oneness.

The fact remains that having a joint account needs high degree of understanding between couples. A lot of people who do not practise it think that it is good but want to avoid rancour that comes from behavioural differences. Likewise, a civil servant in Abia State suggested that joint account should be encouraged for two reasons: (1) where one person is not always around and (2) when they are both earning at the same level. He agreed that the family plans better if there is joint spending and observed that some 'nice' women give their husbands all they earn and it helps the family plan well.

In my interactions with couples, I found several pros and cons of operating a joint account. One major concern is about dishonesty and unfaithfulness, whereby a spouse earns extra money without acknowledging it. Some think that either joint or separate account-keeping is dependent on if the women will let their husbands know how they spend their earnings.

Despite the lapses and issues with joint account, the Bible makes it plain that, 'they two shall be one' (Mark 10:8): One in everything, knowing that money makes or mars the family; in financial transactions, oneness must be entrenched. As long as there is truthfulness, sincerity, carefulness and emotional stability, a couple can succeed in running a joint account. For couples about to marry, it is best to build a solid foundation for a stable family. If the two disagree on such a fundamental issue during courtship, it will be difficult to agree on other major issues of life. As Christians, this calls for a rethink of the relationship before setting out for marriage. From personal experience, I know that joint account works and is a safe haven for the family, especially when the going gets tough.

The family should prayerfully plan the use of their monthly earning. Budgeting is very important in a Christian home. Proper budgeting enables one to estimate how much family income and expenditure there is. Knowing that we are accountable to God for every money we spend as good stewards in His vineyard, we should plan ahead and discipline ourselves in spending. This will enable us to cultivate a habit of planned-giving. Apparently, in the midst of hardship, economic recession and high rate of inflation, it becomes extremely difficult to plan ahead. However, Christians are encouraged to honestly work hard and prayerfully approach their daily financial transactions. After all, the word of God promises us that '…my God shall supply all your needs according to His riches in glory by Christ Jesus' (Philippians 4:19).

A joint account does not necessarily mean having a bank account, but is the principle of spending from the same purse. It is a call on the husband and his wife to declare all their income and plan together to spend as one. It is a willingness to acknowledge all they have and sincerely offer everything for the welfare of the household. It makes for better planning and smoother running of the affairs of the home. Mbanaso (1997) states that "each couple have got to sit down, fast and pray when they get their salary, plan under God how best to use it. If this is not done, there will be great suspicion and untrustworthiness about how money is being used.' Finally, running finances together is the best design for Christian families and it removes unnecessary pressures from the family.

Chapter 6

MINISTERING IN THE CHURCH

Modupe has been a prayer band leader for the youth group of her church for six years before her marriage to Bankole. She got married and continued to function as prayer band leader. Her husband was quite happy to let her attend prayer meetings, until she went to the extreme. Bankole's complaint is that his wife fasts almost every day and does not have adequate strength to go about her domestic duties. She is hardly cheerful and feels that he is not in any way part of what she is doing and so should not interfere. On the other hand, Bankole was very busy ministering with a gospel music band in town. It has become difficult for these two to stay and share together what the Lord is doing in their family. By the time I met Bankole, he was far from happy. He was quite irritable, feeling that they could live separately even while still married. For him, living with Modupe has become a challenge.

> And the Lord said, 'It is not good that the man should be alone; I will make him a help meet for him'. *Genesis 2:18*

After reading the above passage, I was ready to take Modupe to task. So I began to speak to her. She was indeed a 'super-spiritual' sister who could not minister along with her husband. But I said to her, 'It is not good that the man, Bankole, should stay alone. Therefore, the Lord made him

Dupe to be a help suitable for him". I asked her, 'Why don't you share in the responsibility of ministering with him?' She answered that she prayed for him and shared the Word of God with him. 'But do you complement him in the ministry? Do you make up for those things he alone cannot do?' These were questions to which she could not give any positive answer.

In Fine Arts, two complementary colours are the colours that are directly opposite each other on the colour wheel[12]. One significance of complementary colours is that, though they look quite contrasting in appearance, they match in any design. This is due to the fact that in a harmonious multi-colour design, bright colours and dark colours ought to be present. Therefore, since green is dull and cool, red complements it with all its brightness and strength. This is the case with orange and blue, purple and yellow. The strength of a design is in the ability of the designer to successfully combine colours that would otherwise be at variance. This is the case in marriage. The ability of the couple to bring out the strength of one another without conflict is the success of marriage.

After several prayer sessions and counselling, Modupe and Bankole were able to resolve their differences and, today, Bankole has a musical band and his wife is his assistant. They now attend many weddings ceremonies, where he ministers in music and she bakes the cake. She is now very approachable and friendly. She understood that she has signed to live as one with Bankole despite his shortcomings. She has also become very humble and cognisant of her own humanness and God's vision for her family.

Nneka and Obinna have been married for ten years before he told her that he was getting the feeling that convinced him that the Lord might someday want him to go into the ordained ministry. During a family retreat, he recounted to her God's dealing with him and how he had been reluctant to accept the call. Nneka became very moody and refused to say anything, whether negative or positive. After two years, she had not given her consent. Obinna got more and more restless. Eventually, she gave a verbal consent but felt that she should not be part of that ministry arrangement at all. Obinna is now ordained as a pastor, but his wife is neither proud of his vocation nor is she willing to work with the church women among whom she finds herself. She does not want to discourage her husband either. The situation is still a prayer topic. Perhaps, one of these days Nneka will be touched.

The Lord actually has shown that He has need of Obinna. The problem here is that the women in the church hardly know their pastor's wife, as she cannot be reached. Sometimes when there are purely women problems, they cannot find someone to help them and yet their pastor is married. But we are told to bear one another's burden. It is not good for the man to bear it alone or with a reluctant partner. This was why Amos 3:3 asks: "Can two walk together except they be agreed?' No, it is not possible.

Back in high school, we used to participate in the three-legged race, in which two persons are tied together with a rope, one right and one left leg and asked to run to a designated post. Usually, if the two are in agreement and have equal strength and determination, they will run evenly and win the race. But those who are not in agreement and who are not well coordinated soon fall on the field and spectators will laugh at them. It is all very exciting. That explains the issue of a couple walking in harmony. A pastor and his wife should be able to walk in unity. They should be enthusiastic about each other so much that they will walk in one accord. As it is in other laudable ventures, this is not easy. As very intelligent people with different aspirations, we want to know what each other is doing. When people come to the home for consultation, a wife should be able to assist her husband when necessary. She should be able to pray for them, email, write, call or visit them on her husband's behalf.

Life is often very difficult for wives of pastors, especially the busy ones, if they are not able to share in their husband's ministry. The result could be that the man is shut out completely from the family due to busy schedules, but if his wife is able to help by writing letters, preparing study guides, teaching some youth groups, attending some ceremonies on his behalf and tidying up books and working materials, life becomes easy for the family.

Marriage is a triangle; each passing year should bring the couple closer to each other. If a wife is a children evangelist and wants to have the children come in to play in their home once a week, she should seek her husband's approval; they should be in agreement, having open doors for that form of ministry at home.

If the Lord calls us to accomplish a task, it is easy to achieve in harmony through praying together as a couple. When the husband is preaching at any programme, his wife should go with him, for three main reasons: to give him moral support, to pray for him while he preaches, and to assess his messages from an unbiased listener's point of view. All these would help him improve year after year. This also applies when the wife goes out to minister. Moreover, the good example of the Christian couple, especially of ministers, will affect the families of other believers and even draw them closer to the Lord Jesus Christ.

Chapter 7

PASTORING TOGETHER

A pastor is a minister in charge of a church or congregation and exercises spiritual guidance over them. He is charged with the spiritual welfare of a group of people who are known as his congregation or flock, just as a shepherd sees to the physical welfare of his sheep. The word 'pastor' appears only once in the King James Version of the Bible in Jeremiah 17: 16 and means, a feeder of sheep. In John chapter 10, Jesus referred to himself as the good shepherd who gives His life for his sheep. This good shepherd is a pastor and a part of his flock. He is touched by their feelings and reaches God on their behalf. His wife should be a willing assistant to him in this business—the task of keeping God's flock intact. Whether this pastor is ordained or not, it is still their first responsibility. Not all pastors are theologians but all should be committed to the safekeeping of God's flock. One can have an effective ministry without any form of theological education or priesthood ordination. What a pastor needs is to be faithful, and live in consecration and commitment to service. The pastor's wife as a co-worker must play her own part cheerfully so that the flock can be edified.

I remember a friend of mine, who was an older pastor's wife, complaining aloud one day. 'I am just tired of this kind of work' she said. 'A work that nobody ever notice, how much more appreciate what you are doing'. 'Mama, but the Lord sees and rewards all our good deeds,' I consoled. 'But my dear, we need the church to encourage us, so that we can do more,' she retorted. 'It is true. But where they do not, let us be sure that we cheerfully perform a good deed,' I encouraged her.

This woman was making a candid point but she was also complaining and so needed to be redirected. She complained of having to trek long distances because they lacked the means of transport; yet, she had so many activities at which she must always be present. Besides, she was often insulted, even though she did not get any kind of incentive for many years. These are some of the discouragements an assistant or deputy always has to face. She is hardly noticed or acknowledged, even when her job is overwhelming.

Not many of us remember that aspect of the ministry. We do not have to be applauded in order to work harder. It is only a person who is not called or who does not understand his or her call that will wait for the encouragement or ovation of people. It is God who has called us to brokenness; he is, therefore, able to uphold us. I told my friend that 'if you waited for so many years to be convinced to marry a pastor, then those years should have taught you life lessons. So you should abide in your calling, working as unto the Lord'. Her problem, I understood, was the absence of real conviction of God's special calling upon her life.

Jesus did not wait to be rewarded with allowances to travel to Jerusalem to preach the gospel. Paul was a missionary, preaching from city to city. Yet he found time to make tents to support himself in the ministry. He did not want to be a burden to the people of God. There was so much zeal and desire within him and these caused him sleepless nights while he prepared to proclaim the gospel.

The life of a pastor's wife must be that of sacrifice and consecration, laid bare before the Lord. Her part is to encourage her husband, who must not be discouraged or fed up with the challenges of the ministry. Together, they should renew each other by the strength of support they provide. Many times, everything looks rosy from afar off; hence, the saying: 'all that glitters is not gold.' Being a leader among women might appear an enviable position. Many may be interested in the honour but will not remember the cross to bear.

A pastor's wife must be a willing worker and a prayerful woman who studies and knows her Bible; one who is committed to training other women, and in whose lifestyle there is no pretence; one whose thoughts are as good as her words, and not a hypocrite in anyway. She needs to be a respectful woman both to her husband and others around, as well as teach her children to respect people. She must not be covetous but generous and accommodating.

Boma was a local politician in her village. But somehow, she got married to a dear humble pastor serving in one of the churches. It has been twenty years or more now and she has remained in politics even as a pastor's wife. Boma must be at the centre of every policy decision, so she attends all committee meetings for both church and community, sometimes uninvited. She is a member of some kind of political party and brings her husband into controversy wherever they are pastoring. She does not understand her role in her husband's pastoral ministry. The wife of a minister must share his vision and aspirations with total commitment. There should not be communication gap between the pastor and his wife. The Bible says that 'her desire should be to please her husband' (Gen. 3:16b).

The woman must know that she is called along with her husband and that her family must be a shining example for the household of God and beyond. Her husband had answered to this following charge at his ordination: 'Will you be diligent to frame and fashion your own self, and your family, according to the doctrine of Christ; and to make both yourself and them, as much as in you lieth wholesome examples and patterns to the flock of Christ?" This ministry is therefore not the sole affair of the pastor but also that of everyone within his family (Appendix C).

The pastor's wife must be serious-minded, temperate and dedicated, not given to malicious tale-bearing. She must be a good example of self-control, keeping her body in temperance, sobriety and charity. She must not be given to wine or any strong drink, because 'when wine enters, the senses go out,' as our people say. She must be such that can hold her tongue, not a gossip, a slanderer or a false witness. She must be faithful in all things.

I was told recently of a pastor's wife who was in charge of the cooking in their church. Her assistant, a lay woman, had gone to the market to buy a bag of rice for cooking in a particular church function. They also bought meat and other ingredients and kept them in the parsonage kitchen. In the morning when they came back to start cooking, this pastor's wife had hidden away a portion of that rice, leaving about three quarters and the bag was not properly tied back. All the ingredients were also reduced. The assistant who went to the market brought up the issue and began to quarrel over it. But the pastor's wife maintained that she had a right to keep some of the rice for her family. This is the height of covetousness. It is not expected of a Christian woman, much less a pastor's wife, to rip-off anyone in whatever form. The women began to look at her as a greedy person. Indeed, they could have used their discretion to give the pastor's household some of the items as gifts, but her show of shame affected such gestures.

The above situation is such that people got to know of the shameful act of this pastor's wife. Many incidents abound in which privately, a pastor's wife is entrusted with money or other property, but which she appropriated to herself or her family. Can the Lord find us faithful? The Christian woman must be honest in the handling of finances and a faithful steward in deed. The Bible says 'Better is a little with the fear of the Lord than great treasure and trouble with it' (Prov. 15:16) and 'He who is greedy for unjust gain makes trouble for his household, but he who hates bribe will live" (Prov. 15:27).

The parsonage (or pastor's house) is a home for all. Therefore, the pastor's wife must be hospitable. She must be ready and willing to entertain guests. However, she must do this wisely, taking into consideration her family and her health. She should ensure that her husband and children are well-fed and that they rest adequately daily.

The responsibilities of today's pastor's wife include leading women and youth organizations and helping in the Sunday school. She must be a good counsellor, a teacher of the word and an administrator in her own right. She should inculcate humility and domesticity into the women and girls of her church. She is the mother of all in the church.

In her relationship with her husband's co-workers, she must be a respectable woman. She must not, by her words, actions and inactions, cause tension between her husband and his colleagues. She should maintain a holy and cordial relationship with the opposite sex, keeping her prestige and being faithful to her own husband in all things.

The pastor's wife should dress decently and neatly and not extravagantly. She may not be able to afford the fashion trends in the society, but she should dress sensibly and appropriately. The world should not be her standard for dressing. Cleanliness, tidiness and modesty will do. She must show moderation in her dressing so that members will not be led astray.

The pastor's house must not be a lighthouse, giving light to others while it remains in darkness; or a signpost, pointing others to heaven but refusing to go itself. St. Paul points out in 1 Corinthians 9: 27: 'But I pummel my body and subdue it, lest after preaching to others I, myself should be disqualified.' Let us therefore pray and study the word of God with all diligence, aspiring to make heaven at all costs. This is the heart of all our work.

I do not share in the belief of some that pastors' children are usually rascally, unruly, uncouth and ill-mannered. All I know is that it is easier to see the child of a man of God who is living an indecent life than that of a lay-man, because a city set on a hill cannot be hidden (Matthew 5:14). 'We should therefore not forget the place of importance which many children of pastors have held and are still holding in society. These include John and Charles Wesley of the Methodist Church; Rev. Dr. John Edmund Haggi of the Haggi Institute; Bishops Oluwole and SC Philips of blessed memory; Professor Ayo Banjo, former VC of the University of Ibadan; Dr. Bisi Sowunmi of the University of Ibadan; Dr. Christopher Dayo Famewo of the University College Hospital, Ibadan; Rev. Dr. Akinwumi Akinyemi; Bolaji Akinyemi, former Nigerian minister of external affairs; Rt. Rev. Prof. E.U. Iheagwam of the Egbu Diocese; and Mrs. Dora Chinyere Nwankiti of blessed memory. These are just a few parsonage children. Pastors' wives should, therefore, brace up to the fact that they help build godly children. Our children can be shining examples of individuals with godly foundation. They have all the facilities to have the best upbringing. The Lord is loving and faithful. He will see his people through.

Chapter 8

AS LIGHT IN THE SOCIETY

Pedro was very popular in the city. He was often seen in the company of friends at work and in church, smiling and making fun. He was quite humorous and much gifted. Pedro had a charisma that made everybody agree with him when he spoke, whether in seminars and workshops or on the pulpit. He was exceptionally good. I had known him for a year before an opportunity for a conversation arose.

'Brother Pedro, how are you?'

'I am fine,' he said, 'What about you?'

'It is well,' I smiled back, 'Hmm, brother, what about your wife and children?'

It took him some unusual moment to respond. His broad smile faded and he seemed taken aback. That appeared not to have been just an innocent question, I thought.

'They are all fine,' he answered at last. 'Do you know my wife?'

'No, but I guess she must be somewhere.' I replied. 'Where is your family?'

'They are home in our village with my parents.'

'And you are here enjoying yourself in this faraway city. How does it feel?'

I find it hard to comprehend why some men would refuse to bring their families over to where they are living and I made it clear to Pedro that this was not a good idea. His case is, however, not an exception. He was one among many who feel that to live with their wives and children would be inconveniencing. He chose the option of travelling home from time to time to see his family members who should live with him.

In our discussion, I later discovered that his wife was married for him on his behalf through his parents and since then, the parents have been in control, deciding what happens in their matrimonial home. Nkechi has never been close to Pedro and he had felt weighed down from the first day. After he became a Christian, he desired to find out the purpose for living and believed that he could not discover it in the midst of his home crowd. He had three children, who lived at home with his wife. It was actually more convenient that way, but....

'Yes, there is a 'but' to it,' I retorted. 'You cannot live a fulfilled life without properly overseeing your family as a father.'

'If anyone does not provide for his relatives and especially for his immediate family, he has denied the faith and is worse than an unbeliever' (1 Tim 5:8 NIV). You have to provide for them physically, materially, spiritually, socially and emotionally. There is no way a father can shy away from these responsibilities and still please God. Running far away will only complicate the problem and cause regrets in the future. Many men who have lived away from their families in their formative years have retired to force themselves on family members who have not bonded with them. There is no fraternal relationship between them.

I know of a man who retired and joined his family in the village after more than thirty years in Lagos. A few months later, his wife left them and went to live alone in Lagos. The elderly man is still shrugging it out at home. It is not right to ignore the stage of active participation in your children's upbringing, when your spouse craved your help and comfort.

Pedro eventually brought his wife and three children to the city but the task to adjust was a bit difficult. It might take time, but it is important that we take the right step. May God perfect all that concerns us, Amen! The Christian family can only shine the light for the society to see if they live in love and unity. It should be a contagious kind of exemplary life that draws others to Christ.

Christian couples should always have the desire to stay together. The story was told of a man of God who was allocated an office in his church premises and he decided to provide a table and a chair for his wife who had just retired as a school teacher. When people came for any business with her husband, she was right there and ready to contribute to their discussion. Many of the parishioners were not pleased with that arrangement and did not hide it from them; but the pastor never told his wife to leave his office. He felt that they were one and ought to be seen as such. I am not in a position to judge this action, but I must confess that there are some advantages in it. We can draw some lessons from this man's example. He is a true man in whom there is no guile. He did not hide anything from his wife. He let her feel that she was a contributor in all he did, so they could harmonize their opinions. Again, he got away from diverse temptations by keeping an open door. A lot of insight could be drawn from his lifestyle. This shows that he respected his wife a great deal. Nevertheless, a couple should allow space for one another's individuality, without an iota of suspicion.

Not many wives would enjoy sitting in the same office with their husbands, especially if one is not the office kind of person. But it is a good idea to stay together at all times. Sometimes, either the wife or husband can have something to hide or protect, but lay aside every form of hypocrisy and be really open to the other person. There should be no secrecy, since they are one.

Many men like to travel from one part of the world to another. Some of them have family members who have never been outside the confines of their villages. Okon was a minister in one of the non-denominational ministries and was an itinerant evangelist. He travelled in and out of the country and that kept him away from his family for the greater part of the year. One day, Femi, a colleague of his, met him at the airport with one of his 'prayer partners' waiting to board an aircraft to travel. Femi asked him if his companion was his wife. Okon said 'No.' 'Then why do you like to travel with her so often?' he queried. 'This is about the third time I have met you together on a trip. 'Oh! She is very prayerful and supports me in prayers all through my ministrations,' he answered.

He was not ashamed until Femi spoke. Femi was very angry with him. He advised him in clear language to stop the questionable behaviour. His wife was at home housekeeping and he was out travelling with a 'prayerful' woman. How could their marriage be a happy one? This was totally unacceptable. Why couldn't he help his wife to build up herself spiritually? How could he be guiltless before God? 'Brother, check your life!' were Femi's final words. Okon's marriage eventually packed up, unfortunately.

I thank God for wives who are so understanding and willing to stay at home without questioning. But it is a wrong approach to supporting your husband. Keeping mute to his excesses will only destroy him. The wife is there to provide counsel that even his mother cannot give. If you keep quiet and he gets into sin and destruction, you have not played your part.

> Son of man, I have made you a watchman for the people of Israel; so hear the word I speak and give them warning from me. When I say to the wicked, 'You wicked person, you will surely die,' and you do not speak out to dissuade them from their ways, that wicked person will die for their sin, and I will hold you accountable for their blood. But if you do warn the wicked person to turn from their ways and they do not do so, they will die for their sin, though you yourself will be saved. *Ezekiel 33:7 – 9*

It is necessary for two people who love and are truly proud of each other to get married for several reasons. One of these reasons is so that they can represent each other when the need arises. When there are several invitations to events, a couple should be able to work it out in such a way that they cover grounds. When this happens, my husband could attend one occasion, while I attend the other and we feel adequately represented. We discuss a lot, so much that at the end of the day it appears as if we were at the same functions. On the other hand, we could send apologies to some and decide on the most important place to be.

When the wife or the husband ought to travel or go out alone, this should be understood and encouraged. On the other hand, a husband or wife should not suspect the movement of his or her partner. A partner does not have to take advantage of the other's trust. A husband should encourage his wife to make outstanding contributions to the society. This could be done if he insists on helping her develop her creative abilities. Many women are very creative and need to be appreciated so they can do better.

> Yes, it takes a mature man to allow his wife to do more than live in his shadow all her life. Mature men are happier people by far, and the types of women they produce feel no need to walk the street and wave sign, demanding their right. They've already got them.[15]

To walk together in the society means that the couple are not to be a disgrace to each other. We often hear of a wife who steals in the marketplace or a husband who gets drunk in the street. These are far from shining as light; and are not good ambassadors of their families. Even where the wife or husband is not a believer, there should be tolerance and love in the relationship so that one can win the other to Christ. The couple should be able to make their mark in the society by being what God wants them to be and not by fighting or struggling with one another.

Staying Apart

It is natural for a husband and wife to live together and stay together at all times. These are two people who are spiritually and emotionally attached to each other. Saint Paul says in 1 Corinthians 7:5:

> Defraud ye not one the other, except it be with consent for a time, that ye may give yourselves to fasting and praying, and come together again, that Satan tempt you not for your inconsistency.

Paul was speaking to husbands and wives who would not oblige each other at all times. The only reason he gave, for which a couple could stay apart, is spiritual: that of prayer and fasting and this must be with consent and in agreement between the two. This does not mean they should stay apart from each other.

Sometime ago, a pastor was counselling a couple about to marry. The elderly man spoke of his personal experience in sincerity and said, 'Make sure you do not at any time live apart. Wait for her to graduate before you wed. Then keep living together'. He advised. 'I am a man of God, by his grace. I love my wife so dearly, but when she was abroad for six months and I was left alone at home, I was an emotional wreck. I tell you, I almost fell into sin." He said that it was God who delivered him and he travelled at the end of six months to join his wife and they eventually returned home together.

There are several reasons that may necessitate a couple to stay away from each other. The most common is the demand of academic work. One of them may need to go to university or college far from their home and this may require staying away for many months. Another reason may be official tour or conference, which might require one person to be away for some time. These are common reasons, among others.

Any time a husband and wife stay apart, it is not very easy for them to stay alone, because their time gets shared with other people. With a couple who love each other, it is quite boring and uninteresting. For those who are not very much in love, it might be a welcome relief. It could create an opportunity for them to bring in other people to share their time with them. This may create tension for the marriage later.

If a Christian couple find themselves living apart for a period, they should spend ample time praying for each other. If the husband is in school and the wife is at home with the children, it will be ideal to visit often, and also exchange letters regularly. Some also phone and email one another on a regular basis. In today's technological age, video calls through Facebook, WhatsApp, Skype, Google Hangout and so on can help bridge the communication gap on a daily basis. We can, through these, pray together online and share recent developments. It is good to share scriptures together and pray on the same items. This can be done by fixing particular dates for praying and fasting and sharing the same topics even though you are apart. It is good to be faithful to this arrangement.

When a couple come together, it is expected that they make up for the days apart. The loving couple will always look forward to the reunion. This should be celebrated. Anytime a husband is away for more than a day, his return should be a thing of great joy. I am not in the position to teach you how to express yourselves, lest it becomes artificial or mechanical. If your desire to stay together is not enough to cause a celebration of each other's return, then re-examine your relationship.

It should cause the wife to cook his best meal and await his return or the husband to take her out for a good time soon after she returns. A show of affection should follow the reunion. The children should also share in rejoicing that the family is together again. Let the children see that it is a good thing. Joy is contagious. They should understand that mom and dad love them. This should be the case, no matter how regularly one travels.

Coming together requires a retreat. It is time to reassess family priorities, pray together and discover how far the Lord has led you in your calling, and share testimonies of the Lord's dealings with the family. The retreat should incorporate Bible studies, prayers and worship. These build the family and make up for the time apart (See Appendix A). Some Christian groups or denominations insist on having retreats for their workers and spouses at some point every year. The aim is to bring the couple closer to each other despite individual schedules. It is possible that both husband and wife are busy with their duties in the church. Each week, there is a line-up of activities. They both keep giving out. It is possible for them to burn out spiritually and begin to feel frustrated with the work. This is because of the absence of renewal and rest. Ministers' retreats can take adequate care of burnout.

Activities that can make up the programme include: Bible studies, prayers, seminars, symposia, rest, games, eating and drinking. A quiet environment is best with gifted ministers from within as resource persons. Members of the group are best suited to challenge others at such programmes. Allow God to lead you into great truths to help your marriage in the midst of busy schedules. It is important not to allow busy schedules to keep you away from each other. (See Appendix B and Appendix D)

Chapter 9

MISFITS IN THE MINISTRY

Some of you young men need to be reminded that not all cutlasses that went to the farm are used. Some just don't cut that deep. A man is not a man simply because he parades an okra sprout… (Zulu Sofola's Wedlock of the Gods)

'A hood does not make a monk' is an old saying. In the same vein, the fact that someone holds a certificate does not really mean that he is properly educated, nor is everyone who goes to church a Christian. One's claim has to be defended in his daily living.

Ndidi was extremely active in the youth group, but who was not very lucky in her marriage, because in her zeal and fervent desire to marry a man of God, she got married to a 'pastor' whom she knew very little about. Pastor Tennyson was one of those who got into the ministry because they had been advised by their parents to do so. His parents wanted one of their six sons to become an ordained minister, because they wanted an enhancement of their religious status.

Ndidi was sincere in her desire but lacked knowledge of scriptures. For that reason, she could not discern that Tennyson was not a sincere Christian. With time, she came to discover that he was living a disorderly life. He told lies without limits, was very arrogant, had inordinate ambitions, was not prayerful and was extremely covetous. She got really discouraged by his hypocritical approach to the Christian faith. As a result, there was no more trust in their relationship, as his activities made her ashamed to relate to members of their church.

Consequently, Ndidi learnt to pray for him and began to insist that they pray together from time to time. Nevertheless, marriage became a trial to her young faith. She was not happy even though he tried his best to keep her happy with material gifts and provisions. She was convinced that they were deceiving themselves and the people of God by this cosmetic approach to ministry. Therefore, she could not submit to him in the ministry, as he defrauded the church at will. He also schemed up ideas to extort money out of his congregants for personal gain. Tennyson knew that he was not called to the vocation and believed that his lot is not to suffer; as such, he competed with the world in eating, drinking and dressing. He was several personalities in one. One night he attended a party in town and his detractors got him drunk, so he was bundled home by his so-called friends, who handed him over to his wife with the sarcastic comment: 'I guess your husband is a wonderful man of God'.

That was it for Ndidi! She broke down and wept sorely. She wished it was a dream, so that she could wake up from the nightmare. It sounded like a movie or theatrical performance; but then she found herself unwillingly involved in a drama and that made it real. This truly patient woman had tried everything to achieve a change of behaviour in her husband but all to no avail. Counselling and prayers were her resort for fifteen years, as she waited for the Lord to visit her husband's ministry; but he only grew worse. Now, it has become too hard to keep coping. She could no longer continue to ridicule herself in the name of a pastor's wife. She decided to advise him to resign from church work. It came to that point because Tennyson was actually a misfit in the ministry. His wife could not continue to watch him mock himself, since 'God cannot be mocked' (Galatians 6:7). He needed the touch of God. She wondered, 'If the Lord had not called him, had he any right to force himself and his 'services' on God?' 'Let us try another occupation', Ndidi advised. 'I can no longer function as a pastor's wife in the haphazard way it is being done here. Let us not destroy ourselves, because the flesh cannot prevail."

Obviously, Tennyson and his like are still in the ministry. But they can do better elsewhere—such as being a public relations officer in a mega business organization, or a mogul with all the business acumen. However, Tennyson neither had the piety nor the message to a world for whom Jesus died. His reputation had been lost and he needed a retreat to discover where he should function.

Tennyson had long left home in pursuit of greener pasture, while Ndidi and their children continue to fend for themselves. Though with much difficulty, Ndidi continues to build her faith.

> Come now and let us reason together, saith the Lord: though your sins be as scarlet, they shall be as white as snow: though they be red as crimson, they shall be as wool. *Isaiah 1:18*

> And I will restore to you the years that the locust hath eaten, the cankerworm and the caterpillar, and the palmerworm, my great army…. *Joel 2:25*

This kind of ministers should come to the Lord in repentance and the Lord shall restore them from backsliding and cause them to be lifted up and given a better position where they actually fit in. 'Return, ye backsliding children, and I will heal your backslidings' (Jeremiah 3:22). Also, it takes a sincere woman to help her husband and vice versa.

> Ye wives, be in subjection to your own husbands; that if any obey not the Word, they also may without the word be won by the conversation of the wives. *I Peter 3:1*

Partial Separation

Why do people become misfits in the ministry? This is the question that I will try to answer in the rest of this chapter. The simple reason there are a lot of unfulfilled ministers today is that many are not fully separated unto Christ. They have not started the race with the true foundation. There could also be a faulty or shaky foundation.

As a starting point, the Lord teaches us to be born again (John 3:3). This is not just semantics but a real experience of transformation through spiritual rebirth. This is the will of God for all who will receive and enter the kingdom of God. For one to partake in the new birth, he or she must be ready to repent and forsake the past life, which is ridden with sin due to the fall of man. By accepting Christ as Lord and personal Saviour, one *receives power to become a child of God* (John 1:12). This also means that *old thing are passed away and all things have become new* in that person's life (II Corinthians 5:17).

This is the reason the Christian faith has transformed nations and broken down the barriers of heathenism, superstition and pagan practices that held the world in bondage in the past. Yet not everyone is saved, because the power is given only to as many as accept Him into their lives. It is expected of a Christian to live a life that is different from that of the world. St. Paul says in 1 Corinthians 6:17, *Come out from among them and be separate*. That separation is crucial to holy living. It is equivalent to consecration, dedication and ordination for service, without which the Christian cannot function adequately.

The next stage is to be thirsty for holy living. The Psalmist says: *As the deer pants after the water brooks, so my soul longs after you* (Psalm 42:1). That thirst and desire for holy living should proceed from deep within anyone who will serve the Lord. There must be a desire for spirituality and this is real through the manifestation of spiritual gifts in the life of a child of God. The fruit of the Spirit will also radiate through one's lifestyle (1 Corinthians 12 and Galatians 5:22, 23).

The next stage involves growing in grace and in the power of His might (2Peter 3:18). This is of paramount importance to a Christian. Spiritual maturity comes with spiritual exercises, just as physical growth follows physical training. In order to grow spiritually, personal and group activities are needed; these include study of scriptures with application and practice of what we learn from the Word of God. At a point when a child of God is steadily growing, the Lord could deem it fit to call him or her to a particular ministry for the edification of the church. The separation of

Paul and Barnabas in Acts 13:2 is a vivid example, as it led to the confirmation of a prophecy and the prayer and blessings of the brethren. They were called at a time of prayer and as the Holy Ghost moved among them.

Service to God is not done by human ability. It must be embarked upon with full persuasion of God's leading and awareness that one cannot do it through eloquence or physical strength. A sincere desire to serve God is essential to surviving the hurdles of the calling. Tennyson missed the mark and it was difficult for him to start afresh. God's own method is very clear and there are no shortcuts to it. One cannot be fulfilled in a ministry into which he called himself. Truly, *the arm of flesh will fail you* – for 'it is not by power or by might, but by the Spirit of God' (Zechariah 4:6). The best way out is to re-examine oneself and turn around. Our God is a God of new beginnings. He will indeed perfect all that concerns you.

Chapter 10

HELPING OTHERS TOGETHER

I served with Beauty in our National Youth Service Corps year. She used to be known as 'Mother in Israel' among us. She was an exquisite lady who was an epitome of generosity and true love, large hearted and extremely accommodating. For most of the service year, it was hard to come to her apartment without meeting guests, either staying overnight, for the weekend or just sharing a meal or two with her.

Recently, I ran into Beauty again after five years. She is now happily married to Benson, a real blessing to her. My singular interest was to inquire how she has adjusted her generosity in her own growing family. Her simple story went thus: 'Ah! It's been five years of actual adjustments. I came into my matrimonial home with my usual plan-less hospitality and soon discovered that we all had to go hungry. My dear, it was not easy for us at first,' she narrated, 'but you know what? Ben was no better. Initially, he complained that I spent too much, but we soon discovered that we were the same. He is generous to a fault, as far as I am concerned. The only sane thing we did was to bring our income together and spend together in a very sincere way.'

'So what was the result?' I asked.

'Marvellous! It took some time to adjust but we can now be ourselves, still spending a lot but just happy to do that without playing the blame game. We know how much we earn and are able to spend within our means.'

Her answer is amusing but straight to the point. Benson and Beauty were able to remain together in their generosity. They are not affluent but are generous givers, who live for others. They had learnt selflessness from the onset, their maxim being 'It is more blessed to give than to receive' (Acts 20: 35). Giving is a Christian principle, not just for the fun of it but giving in order to help others, as well as to obey the Lord's command. It is the response of true love which is practical and enduring.

In today's society, many give for different motives. Some give in order to receive favour in return, or to show off during fund-raising, when names of donors are announced, as well as during parties, with so much money-spending spree on the celebrants and dancers. Others give to discard what is not useful to them, while some give out of compulsion. As Christian couples, our motives ought to be examined. Some people do not like to give at all. They prefer to live in their own cage, living and working for self. They eventually become victims of suspicion, greed and covetousness.

A dear friend of mine got married to a lady who refused to host any guest in their home. More so, she was sceptical about relatives, with a weird belief that guests and extended family members are a nuisance and posed a threat to her family's economy. Hence, she became hostile and unaccommodating to any guest that came around. This attitude began to create a rift between her and her very benevolent husband. In fact, they had several quarrels because of her defiant stand. For the young man, it was absolutely unchristian and very un-African to distance oneself from one's relatives and community. The desire to keep the nuclear family together should not stop anyone from loving and caring for others and living for them. This is the will of God for His children. It was Robert Wieland who stated:

> We weren't created for the purpose of living for ourselves. Look at the things of nature, everything lives for others. The flowers give their honey for the bees, the rivers flow to water the thirsty land and then to replenish the oceans. The oceans produce the clouds that bring the showers of rain. The sun shines to gladden the darkest corner of the forest, the birds sing to give us music. So we find our true purpose in life in giving ourselves for others. This secret of life is taught everywhere in nature. [17]

Jesus came to earth to die that we may have life (John 10:10). It was His mission to give Himself as a ransom for us. Now we are set free. We are believers, called to serve. That is our task, to do good at all times because the Lord has called us as 'light of the world'. God said to Abraham in Genesis 12:3, 'in thee shall all families on earth be blessed." You should let other families be blessed through you. The Girl Guides would say, "A guide is a friend to all and a sister to every other Guide.' What about a Christian? A Christian should help the homeless, the destitute; visit the sick, give to the needy, and teach the ignorant— doing it all heartily, not occupying our hearts with materialism, which never leads to contentment. The 'I' syndrome is very dangerous and you ought to beware of it. The Lord requires us to surrender fully to Him. He has designed that you should give back one-tenth of your earning to Him as a mark of total surrender. The issue of giving one-tenth, otherwise known as tithing, can be found in the following passages of scriptures: Leviticus 27:30 – 33; Numbers 18:20 – 24; I Corinthians 9:8 – 14; Matthew 23:23; Malachi 3:10,12. A couple should learn to faithfully do this. The testimony of many such families is that the Lord has always remained faithful in prospering them. Those that do this will hardly have discord, because they have put the Lord first by returning tithes and offerings to Him.

Another means of helping people is by giving meaningful time to praying for others and guiding those who need our direction; or by finding time to do some of the odd jobs in the church. It is good to work without being noticed; the Lord honours such workers and rewards them abundantly. When I lived on campus as an undergraduate, our Christian Union (CU) owned several buses which were usually parked in front of the CU Secretariat in the halls of residence. On a particular year, one of the buses, which were used on a daily basis, was found to be washed and clean every morning. For weeks and months, the washing was done long before anyone woke up; the washer was careful to do the task in secret. At a point, the CU president set up a vigilante group to know this nocturnal workman, and he was finally known. This humble brother was openly recognized at his send-forth ceremony, which was embarrassing to him, as he had thought no one (but God) knew of his work. Indeed, God rewarded him bountifully long after he graduated.

Couples could do a lot of good deeds, without wanting to be noticed or applauded. If you give money to your parents, you do not call your brothers and sisters to let them know how well you are taking care of them! If you see to the welfare of a certain indoor member of your church, do you write his or her name in your report so that the entire church or diocese can know how much you saved the person from dying by your philanthropy? What do you hope to achieve by that? If you give hypocritically, know that you have no reward from God. Our daily work should be to cause others to know the Lord fully.

It is by the giving habit of parents that their children learn to give and eventually grow up to look after their own families, parents inclusive. The Igbos say that when a mother goat is eating leaves, the baby goat watches to learn which leaves are edible. We must also find time to be of help to our neighbours in order to bring them to Christ— such time includes that spent on witnessing and winning souls to the Lord.

Chapter 11

SETTLING IN-HOUSE PROBLEMS

When two persons live together, it is natural to have friction and disagreement, because no two individuals are exactly the same. Even two identical twins do not think and act alike at all times. For this reasons, individuals should learn how to relate with others in order to avoid tension, bitterness and malice. It is expedient to give room for others to express themselves even when it appears to hurt. The Bible says in Ephesians 4:26: *Be angry but sin not, let not the sun go down on your anger.* Thus, Christian couples should learn to make up their differences immediately to prevent relationships from deterioration.

In-house matters or domestic issues are peculiar to a couple and their home. There are various causes of in-house frictions. It is possible for a spouse to feel that there is a problem, while the other thinks differently. Nevertheless, once there is such a feeling, the issues need to be addressed. As the saying goes, 'nothing should be swept under the carpet," because the trash would definitely resurface later. A nonchalant attitude to one person's feeling will only lead to deeper ill-feelings. Apparently, tension in the home is created by disagreement between spouses on both simple and complex issues. Inadequate finance and material resources, however, seems to top the list of such issues, followed by prayerlessness, carnality, presence of new persons in the household, ill-health, etc.

We belong to an age in which people love to advance in their society. Most young people believe that the sky is their limit in all endeavours. There could be disagreement on choices, like where to live, what job to do, returning to school for further studies, the number of babies to have, and method of birth control to adopt. If such matters are not approached prayerfully, they can leave permanent scars on the matrimonial life. It takes love and the absence of competition between the husband and wife to be able to settle such disagreements amicably whenever they occur.

Obviously, inadequate finance adversely affects families. Only a minute number of families are always buoyant in their resources all through life. That is why the traditional marriage vows say: 'for richer, for poorer, in sickness and in health, till death us do part." With knowledge of this vow, it is easy to cope in every situation, knowing that the Lord will always make a way out for His children. Unfortunately, not much is being said today about godliness with contentment, which the Bible says is great gain. For this reason, most people find it difficult to handle periods of financial crisis. Sometimes, a woman knows that the family account is exhausted for the month, yet she is desiring new clothes for a special occasion. If there is no money, a couple should be sincere enough with each other in discussing their finances and finding ways and means of managing what they have left.

When the Federal Government of Nigeria came up with its so-called 'austerity measures' of the 1980s, a lot of protests ensued, as people found it difficult to accept the measures. But there was no way out, since the economy was already bad. Things soon became worse as a result of corruption and financial recklessness of government. They then instituted the Structural Adjustment Programme (SAP), which led to more riots and industrial strikes, resulting in closure of universities and colleges and bringing the economy to a standstill. But at the end, everyone had to face the reality— there has to be some kind of 'adjustment' if people must survive the harsh economic environment; hence, SAP came to stay.

Certainly, financial problems do not call for fighting. Couples should pray to God for a way out of poverty and stress, as these are never meant to be permanent situations. The scripture makes it clear in Philippians 4:19: 'but my God shall supply all your needs according to his riches in glory by Christ Jesus.' If that is the case, then it is good to have faith that soon these problems will be over, than to break down the family during trying times. It is time to creatively explore ways of generating additional resources for your family. What are your talents and interests? Network with other believers and approach your problem with ingenuity. Work diligently to set your family up for success; for 'faith without works is dead' (James 2:14). Pray hard, but work relentlessly for your financial turnaround.

When there are extra persons in the house, additional tension may arise. Sometimes, a house-help who is not pleased with the volume of house chores could decide to be uncooperative and disruptive, thereby adding to the stresses in the home. Of course, individual and family prayers will be the approach to solving problems. On the other hand, if you find that the family is unable to accommodate, you should agree to keep the number of guests your home can manage, because the devil can destroy relationships through human agents. These agents may not be conscious of what they are doing, but have the ability to negatively impact families, especially, where they are not prayerful enough to discern and counter what is happening.

An unspiritual partner may be a thorn in the flesh of his/her partner, thus dragging the other down in spiritual matters. A husband may want to spend his time fasting and praying, attending retreats, Bible studies, and Christian seminars to enable him to grow in the faith; meanwhile, his wife may not be too keen on all these, or vice versa. The other persons may be out there hustling, pursuing the things of the world, without seeking first the kingdom of God and His righteousness, thereby leading to procrastination of God's agenda. The result would be spiritual blindness and lack of joy. Apparently, whichever partner is in tune with God at any point in time should make effort to lend a helping hand to the other. Encourage one another through prayer and righteous living. If your spouse was a true Christian but has begun to backslide, tell him or her in clear terms to sit up without being hypocritical: 'Bear one another's burden and so fulfil the law of Christ' (Galatians 6:2).

The best approach to solving a marital problem is not preaching at each other. A man may be over-defensive and will not accept being at fault, especially if his wife is passing judgement on him. It is not advisable to go about preaching at and condemning your spouse. But does this mean you should invite an outsider for help? That could only be a last resort. When the third person gets into your relationship to settle between the two of you, your marriage would receive a crack and would need more work to restore. If you do that, you further become distanced from each other. After all, the Bible says: *And the two shall become one* (Genesis 2:24). Do people settle problems between you and yourself? If the answer is no, then know that it is appalling to invite outsiders to settle your in-house problems for you. An Igbo adage says that you do not obtain friendship by settling disputes. As much as possible, you should learn to handle your problems prayerfully and reconcile yourselves before it gets to the point of inviting a third party.

However, when a marriage relationship is breaking down because spouses do not listen to each other, then their pastor or marriage counsellor should be involved. It is more important to find help to resolve your disagreements than to continue to fight until it is too late. Each person knows can discern when the situation is out of hand. Especially, when you no longer talk things over, there's anger in your heart and you seem regretful of your marriage. Do not wait until there is an altercation between you. Humbly call out for help! We say NO to violence of any kind. The God of reconciliation is still able to restore your marriage if you act in faith.

While settling disagreements, couples should approach each other with prayer, humility and affection. During most weddings, couples are advised to go into their bedrooms and settle their misunderstandings away from the rest of the world. This is a time-tested, effective method of forging ahead. It is certainly not an unattainable goal. Pride and anger are two types of cankerworms that eat up marriages and should never be allowed to thrive. As most marriages began with love and affection, so they should continue with them. When your husband or wife smiles at you, make sure you acknowledge it and accept it as genuine, remembering the very day you got engaged to each other.

There is also the need to always admit being wrong whenever you are blamed. Even where it hurts you, accept your fault and apologise, and have a desire to make up quickly. Be willing to give in for the sake of reconciliation and restoration of your cordial relationship. This requires humility, which of course is a key Christian virtue we all need for successful marriage. At this point, note that it is very important to believe in your partner's good intentions; that he or she is not interested in merely hurting you and keeping you miserable— for 'charity covers a multitude of sins' (I Peter 4:8). The fact that you love each other should always guide your thoughts towards one another.

A willingness to forgive each other and forget whatever wrongs were done is the remedy for all bitterness. Once a problem has been discussed, each person should forgive and forget the past. Do we not all recite the Lord's Prayer saying, *forgive us our trespasses as we forgive those who trespass against us?* (Matthew 6:12). Evidently, God forgives and forgets and never refers to our past sins, which He has erased by cleansing: for we know that *the blood of Jesus cleanses us from all sin* (I John 1:9). That is why many marriages continue year in, year out, happy and joyful, to the glory of God. May the Lord give us grace to continue in His will.

God ordained marriage for believers and gave us the grace to make it work. Our part is to live in obedience and trust in the Lord to uphold us, because marriage is a lifelong covenant that should be taken seriously. Lewis Swedes, in *Mere Morality*, said:

> Perhaps the greatest mystery of our humanness is the power to make and keep a vow. For in a vow you freely give yourself over to a permanent identity in the face of an unpredictable future. You will change, the person to whom you make the vow will change, and your circumstances will change.[12]

Marriage is a solemn institution. Bearing this in mind, therefore, one should never get married to anyone to whom he or she will not be willing to give up when problems arise. It is a *divorceless* covenant. Remember the declaration at your wedding, 'What God has joined together, let no man put asunder' (Mark 10:9). During a dispute, the only solution is to reason together, solve problems and always positively aspire to succeed together. It is not the time to look around, as many do, for extramarital affairs. There is no success when you leave your husband or wife for another person.

Recent data show that second and third marriages have less success rates than the first (See Appendix F). Divorce is a habit that forms as soon as the first one occurs. Some become polygamists and others become progressive monogamists: they marry, divorce, remarry and yet divorce, thus continuing the unending cycle. However, Jesus explains that the two states are the same:

But I tell you that anyone who divorces his wife, except for sexual immorality, makes her the victim of adultery, and anyone who marries a divorced woman commits adultery. *Matthew 5:32 (NIV)*

Several unresolved matters have caused many to abandon their families for outsiders. That is the way of cowards and escapists. Separation and divorce have never solved marital problems; instead, they have always complicated them. The Christian marriage is without divorce. All you can do is to improve the lot of your partner in whatever way you can. I have heard of many husbands who have felt that their wives no longer meet up to their standards after many years of marriage; hence, they begin to get irritated by her presence. This may lead to health problems, such as psychological disorders, as their husbands head out in waywardness and their children are neglected. Therefore, it is necessary to grow along with your spouse spiritually, academically, politically and otherwise. By so doing, she or he will always fit into your crowd. Otherwise, you will eventually have yourself to blame. Do not be like the pastor who complained that his wife has never been adventurous and, as such, could never learn new ways of life. He ended up living lonely, as he only succeeded in ostracising himself from the rest of his family.

We cannot sacrifice too much for our faith in Jesus Christ. To keep the family intact is a task that every couple must fulfil. Jesus came to reconcile the world to himself and gave us a ministry of reconciliation. Therefore, there is no offence that is beyond resolution. If one has already fallen prey to marital discord, separation or divorce, the way back is through the finished work of Christ on the cross. Repent and be reconciled to God. Go and sin no more. Make up your mind to live righteously henceforth, and the God of marriage will uphold you.

Chapter 12

A CALL TO BROKENNESS BEFORE GOD

Blessed are the poor in spirit for theirs is the kingdom of heaven.
Matthew 5:3

The Dakes Annotated Reference Bible interprets the poor in spirit as the broken spirit.[20] If that is what it means, then we grasp with us the need for brokenness, the need to be melted in one's spirit, to know spiritual poverty, and to understand that it is not by power nor by might but by the Spirit of God that we are called. Therefore, we must live according to His plans.

These are the days of much study and learning. The Preacher in Ecclesiastics 12:12 says: *...of making many books there is no end and much study is a weariness of the flesh.* We see many weary people today who are tired of much study in theology, philosophy, psychology, religion and all forms of humanities. Evidently, except studies are pursued with a broken spirit, they weary the soul. If a person's mind is not teachable, then there is no place for God, because *knowledge puffs up, but love edifies* (1Corinthians 8:1). Numerous men and women are bloated by the philosophies they have acquired and do not find joy and satisfaction because they have missed the real source of joy. Surely, the power of spiritual learning is in the anointing of the Holy Spirit.

How can you experience a broken spirit; a life that is truly surrendered to God? What does that involve? How do you keep being broken even after much learning and acquisition of advanced knowledge? How do you qualify to be part of the kingdom of heaven as someone who is poor in spirit? How do you live to serve God effectively? Jeremiah 18:1 – 11 says:

> The word which came to Jeremiah from the LORD, saying: 'Arise and go down to the potter's house, and there I will cause you to hear My words". Then I went down to the potter's house, and there he was, making something at the wheel. And the vessel that he made of clay was marred in the hand of the potter; so he made it again into another vessel, as it seemed good to the potter to make.
>
> Then the word of the LORD came to me, saying: 'O house of Israel, can I not do with you as this potter?' says the LORD. 'Look, as the clay is in the potter's hand, so are you in My hand, O house of Israel! The instant I speak concerning a nation and concerning a kingdom, to pluck up, to pull down, and to destroy it, if that nation against whom I have spoken turns from its evil, I will relent of the disaster that I thought to bring upon it. And the instant I speak concerning a nation and concerning a kingdom, to build and to plant it, if it does evil in My sight so that it does not obey My voice, then I will relent concerning the good with which I said I would benefit it.
>
> 'Now therefore, speak to the men of Judah and to the inhabitants of Jerusalem, saying, 'Thus says the LORD: 'Behold, I am fashioning a disaster and devising a plan against you. Return now everyone

from his evil way, and make your ways and your doings good.'

The illustration of the potter and the clay given to Jeremiah by the Lord is a classic for all generations of Christians. The Lord explains His dealings with man through his relationship with the house of Israel. He speaks explicitly to us today regarding the contriteness of heart needed now more than ever before. In that passage, Jeremiah is given the sign of the potter at work fashioning clay just the way he wants it to be:

> Then I went down to the potter's house and behold he wrought a work on the wheels. And the vessel that he made of clay was marred in the hand of the potter. So he made it again another vessel as seemed good to the potter to make it. *Jeremiah 18:3-4*

I like pottery a lot. It is an art of expression backed up by a deep creative craving within the artist. A potter verbalizes with the clay whatever he wants to create. The clay is in his hands to refine and make ready for the kind of piece he wants to produce. In preparation for pottery-making, the potter refines the clay. The finer the particles of clay used, the more the plasticity of the object produced. Clay is the plastic ingredient used for modelling forms, such as chinaware, glassware, pots and all forms of sculptural pieces. It is pliable and can hold together. If it is too watery, it loses plasticity; and if it too hard, it loses its pliability.

Consequently, while the potter is preparing the clay he asks himself what kind of piece or design he wants to produce: a teacup, a pot, a bowl, a flower vase, or what? He then sets up the potter's wheel, switches it on, marks out the measurements and begins to work. This is the time to put his skills to work till the article is completed. If the form is not coming up the way he wants, it would take just a finger at the top as he continues to turn the wheel, and the whole clay crumbles into a lump, then he mixes it up again and starts afresh.

Our God is awesome, much greater than this potter who desires to produce befitting articles that will be dignifying to him. God wants wares that have aesthetic and utilitarian values that He can be proud of. This way, our Master Creator, the Almighty God made us in His own image that we might live to glorify His name in all areas of our lives, including marriage and family life.

The Broken and Contrite Heart

The Lord Jesus came to redeem man from the hardness of heart and set him free from the bondage of the devil. Psalm 51:17 says: *a broken and a contrite heart O God, thou wilt not despise.* God will not ignore your brokenness, your humility and repentance. Yet, this is the condition under which you can serve God acceptably; brokenness involves a melted heart with a readiness to accept the work of the Holy Ghost.

Many Christians are set in their ways due to habits, dogmas and parochialism. We are used to some crippling expressions such as, 'I cannot stop it', 'that's the way I was brought up', 'it's our tradition,' 'and I'm too old to learn to use the left hand'. These are dangerous trends for a successful marriage. Indeed, two persons cannot have a fruitful and lasting walk together except these carnal traits are done away with and they become malleable in the hand of God.

The Lord wants to mould us the way the potter does his clay until He is able to obtain the desire of His heart regarding the product. Therefore, we should be willing to be broken as He wants to refine us, using His sieve to remove all the impurities in us until we are pure and plastic enough for His high and holy calling. He always pours into us the water of His Word, so that we can be plied by the Holy Spirit, leading us into all truth. Our task is to be obedient, so that we are not rejected halfway; we are to endure to the end, relying on the sufficiency of His grace towards us.

Sadly, due to hardness of heart and disobedience, which are the handiwork of the devil, many Christian couples are not making it together: they live separate lives and have no good examples to show. They stress through life like rejected clay, too watery or too strong. False doctrines must be watched closely in your spouse, because these days are evil. If your spouse imbibes a false doctrine, you must be quick to prayerfully point it out to him or her, because it can water down the faith and result in a careless lifestyle and nonchalance. The church in Laodicea failed because it was neither hot nor cold (Revelations 3:14 – 19).

Someone can become hard-hearted and, thereby, set in his or her ways. This is a strong red light. A spouse noticing this tendency in the other must pray and cry "Wolf!" because if care is not taken, that person is heading to a reprobate mind-set. The greatest thing you can do for each other is to build up yourselves in the faith. The arguments about whether we should go to Bible studies, retreats, if fasting and praying or night vigil are still relevant or if giving or tithing is important are elementary and should not even constitute a problem for Christians that are ready to move along with the Holy Spirit. The simple answer to these questions and many others is: 'Yes!' So let's plan together to do them according to the will of God.

The Lord never finishes with us. He has loved us with His everlasting love, so the growth process is continuous for believers. According to General Douglas Macarthur:

> Life is a lively process of becoming. If you haven't added to your interest during the past year, if you are thinking the same thought, relating the same personal experiences, having the same predictable reactions, rigor mortis of the personality has set in.[21]

Anyone that has 'stopped' growing is of no use to God, because God cannot have His way in that life or in his or her marriage. The Lord's will for us is to bring us perfect before him. It is the potter who sends his work to the kiln for firing in order to perfect it, thereby achieving aesthetic and utilitarian excellence. The Lord passes us through a growth process, which is sometimes not so pleasurable. It is only a person who undergoes trials successfully like pure gold that becomes an overcomer, having been perfected by God Himself (Revelations 3:21).

All Christian couples should constantly be on guard, searching themselves and surrendering to the Lord, who will give us the power to be His and to work together in harmony. Marriage is a blessing to mankind. It is ordained by God to be a honourable and holy estate; hence, Christian couples ought to maintain their vows to remain with each other. This is the condition for God's blessings upon our lives and ministries, as well as, answered prayers, as stated in I Peter 3:7:

> Likewise, ye husbands, dwell with them according to knowledge, giving honour unto the wife, as unto the weaker vessel, and as being heirs together of the grace of life; that your prayers be not hindered.

References

1. Livingstone, E.A. (1977). *The Concise Oxford Dictionary of the Christian Church*. London: Oxford University Press, pg.83.
2. *The Book of Common Prayer* (1922). The form of solemnization of matrimony. London, SPCK, pg.302.
3. Ibid, p. 302
4. Ibid, p. 303
5. Theodore, H. (1989). *Far Above Rubies.* Jos, Nigeria, Challenge Publications.
6. Llwelyn, J.D. (1986). *Every Woman.* Bungay, Suffolk, Faber and Faber, Richard Clay. The Chaucer Press Ltd. pg.99.
7. Spock, B. and Needlman, R. (2011). *Dr Spock's Baby and Child Care.* 9th edition. New York, pg.29.
8. Llwelyn, J.D. (1986). *Every Woman.* Bungay, Suffolk, Faber and Faber, Richard Clay. The Chaucer Press Ltd. pg.99.
9. Spock, B. and Needlman, R. (2011). *Dr Spock's Baby and Child Care.* 9th edition. New York, pg.29.
10. *Ebony Magazine* (June, 1990). A Johnson publication. Pg.66.
11. Mbanaso, A.U. (1997). Pressure areas of homes and family. *Plumbline Magazine.* Ibadan, Scripture Union (Nigeria). Pg.34.
12. Avae, D.T.M. (1990). *The Essentials of Art.* Idoho Umieh Publishers Ltd, Nigeria. Pg.18.
13. *The Book of Common Prayer.* (1958). The ordering of deacons. London, SPCK. Pg. 566.
14. Arulefela, O. (Unpublished). The pastor's wife. A pamphlet.
15. Hardistry, M. (1979). *Forever My Love.* Eugene Oregon, Harvest House Publishers. Pg.98.
16. Sofola, Z. (1981). *Wedlock of the Gods.* London, Evans Brothers Ltd. Pg.15.
17. Wieland, R.J. (nd). *Marriage in Today's World.* Osu Accra. Advents Press. Pg.79.
18. *Book of Common Prayer.* (1958). order of holy matrimony. London, SPCK. Pg. 303.
19. Allan, P.J. (1973). *For Men Only.* Wheaton Illinois, Tyndale House Publishers.

20. Dake, F.J. (1989). *Dakes Annotated Reference Bible*. Dake Bible, USA, Sales Inc. Lawrenceville, GA. Pg.4.

21. Allan, P.J. (1973). *For Men Only*. Wheaton Illinois, Tyndale House Publishers.

22. *Thy Kingdom Come* (1997). Seminar paper published by SU (Nigeria). Pg.4.

23. Ononiwu, I. (1998). *Jewels for My Dear Wife*. Port Harcourt, Springtime Books. Pg.75.

Bible References
Except otherwise stated, all references are from the Authorized Version of the King James Bible.

CHAPTER ONE
Joshua 24:15a
Acts 9
Revelation 3:20
John 3:16b
Revelation 7:9
Hebrews 12:1
Romans 2:21
1 Corinthians 11:3

CHAPTER TWO
1 Peter 1:15
Philippians 3:10, 11

CHAPTER THREE
Matthew 16:24
Ephesians 5:22, 24
1 Peter 3:1
1 Corinthians 7:4, 33
Proverbs 31: 10, 11, 23
Genesis 19: 1

CHAPTER FOUR
Matthew 19:6, 8:9 – 10
1Peter 4:8

Matthew 18:19

CHAPTER FIVE
Proverbs 22:6
Acts 2:1
Amos 3:3
Joshua 1:8, 4:6, 7
Hebrew 10:25
Galatians 6:1, 2
Luke 11:1
Mark 1:35
Philippians 4:19

CHAPER SIX
Genesis 2:18
Amos 3:3
2Timothy 2:22

CHAPTER SEVEN
Jeremiah 17:16
John 10
Genesis 3:16b
Proverbs 15:16

CHAPTER EIGHT
1Timothy 5:8 (NIV)
Ezekiel 33
1Corinthians 7:5
Proverbs 15:27

1Corinthians 9:27

Matthew 6:14

CHAPTER NINE

Galatians 6:7

Isaiah 1:18

Joel 2:25

1Peter 3:1

John 3:3

John 1:12

2Corinthians 5:17

2Corinthians 6:17

Psalms 42:1

1Corinthians 12

Galatians 5:22, 23

Acts 13:2

Zechariah 4:6

CHAPTER TEN

Acts 20:35

John 10:10

Genesis 12:3

Leviticus 27:30 – 33

Numbers 18:20 – 24

1Corinthians 9:8 – 14

Matthew 23: 23

Malachi 3: 10, 12

CHAPTER ELEVEN

Ephesians 4:26

Philippians 4:19
Galatians 6:2
Genesis 2:24
1 Peter 4:8
Matthew 6:12

CHAPTER TWELVE
Matthew 5:3
Ecclesiastes 12:12
Jeremiah 8:1 – 11
Psalm 51:17
Revelations 3:14 – 19
Revelations 3:21

APPENDIX A

Suggested programme for family retreat

Venue: A homely retreat centre

Time: Start from early morning

Duration: One or more days

Participants: Every member of the family

Ministers: Parents

Assisted by: Children

Activities

1. Opening prayer
2. Worship session
3. Exhortation – The purpose of the solemn gathering
4. Choruses/Hymns
5. Special numbers
6. Choruses
7. Testimonies
8. Prayer session 1 – Prayers of confession and persistence
9. Talk or admonition or participatory Bible study
10. Prayer session II – Individual prayer requests
    - Prayer for the family
    - Other issues
11. Sharing and caring
12. Closing prayer

APPENDIX B

Suggested programme for ministers' families retreat

Venue: A spacious quiet environment

Time: Start on the evening of the first day and end by afternoon of the third day

Participants: All pastors in a particular church, pastor's wives, and pastor's family members.

Officiating ministers: Pastors, children evangelists in the group, any family member that has a message to share.

Activities:
Day One
1.   Arrival and registration
2.   Assemble at the designated chapel
3.   Opening session
    i. Prayers
    ii. Programme distribution
    iii. Instruction on rules of the event
    iv. Introduction of officers
4.   Choruses
5.   Exhortation or talk on the theme
6.   Prayer session
7.   Closing prayers
8.   Supper
9.   Retire for the day/lights out

Day Two (Prayer and fasting day)
    1. Rising up
    2. Individual Quiet time

3. Clean up
4. Morning worship
5. Breakfast for children., the elderly and the sick
6. Bible Study/children's fellowship
7. Prayer hour (lunch for children)
8. Rest
9. Talk
10. Prayer hour
11. Testimonies/special numbers
12. Break
13. Supper
14. Indoor games (all participants)
15. Talk
16. Closing prayer
17. Retire for the day/Lights out

Day Three
1. Rising up
2. Quiet time
3. Clean up
4. Morning worship
5. Breakfast
6. Worship service: Testimonies, talk
7. Concluding session
    - Reassessment of the programme
    - Input for future planning
    - Appreciation
    - Exchange of gifts (if any)
    - Closing prayers/benediction
    - Departure.

APPENDIX C

Family Picnics

1. One, two or more families can decide to plan and execute a picnic or love feast
2. Picnics are merrier if each family would cook and bring their own delicacies for sharing
3. Pastries should be provided, especially for the children
4. Involve children in making face caps, garlands, blowing balloons and preparing for outdoor games
5. Pack your picnic baskets with foods, drinks, fruits, plates, straws, cutleries, and cups. Also come along with mats, camp beds and other materials.
6. Remember that 'unto the Lord shall the gathering of His people be.' Therefore, do not forget your Bible and hymn book.

Venue: A park, zoological garden, lake side, ranch, open field, etc.

Activities: The programme of activities will depend on family interests. There should be time to share experiences, act drama, sing and listen to gospel music, play games and share the word of God. Refreshment should be shared with joy. Picnic is meant for refreshment and renewal of strength. It is a kind of recess. The programme should achieve these.

Warning: Do not plan for a picnic only when you are less busy. In the midst of busy schedules, reduce stress by stealing away to a picnic site.

APPENDIX D

Useful Christian Indoor Games

1. **Who Am I?**

The moderator of the game is to write the names of 2 Bible characters on two separate sheets of paper. Two volunteers will be called up and each will have one of the name-tags fastened on his/her back, e.g. Esther and Job.

The instructions are as follows:

a.   The participant will ask questions such as; 'Am I a man?' 'Is my name in the New Testament?' 'Am I a prophet?' 'Am I Peter?' etc.

b.   The audience must answer YES or NO, nothing more than that is accepted.

c.   The person who guesses the correct name is declared the winner.

   • This game is suitable for youth and adults.

2.   **Passing the Basket**

A basket containing wrapped questions which may include jokes, riddles, current affairs, Bible topics, etc. is passed round the participants from one end to the other.

Music is played at the background as the basket is handed from one person to the other. Anyone holding the basket when the music is stopped is asked to pick one question. He/she is to answer whatever question is read out and the basket continues to move. Anyone who is unable to answer is helped by another person he chooses. Some questions should go with rewards like, biscuits, toffees, toys, etc.

- Suitable for people of all age groups.

3.   Sword Drill

This involves finding passages of the Bible as they are announced by the moderator. Four or more people can participate at a time. The first person to find a Bible verse and read it out is remarked. The recorders record whoever finds it first. Up to ten Bible verses could be called out, at the end of which the persons with the first, second and third positions shall be announced and probably rewarded with prizes.

- Use a Bible version and language that all participants are conversant with.
- Suitable for youth and the young at heart.

4.   God has something to say!

This game involves a group of people who will quote Bible verses which they have memorized. As the song goes on, each person quotes, until individuals begin to give up. The last person to give up emerges the winner.

APPENDIX E

Teaching the family to pray the ACTS way

A – Adoration: Worship, love deeply and respect highly. Psalm 145

C – Confession: Act of admitting or saying that one is wrong or has done wrong. Acknowledging one's doing, especially sin committed. Psalm 51, 1John 1:8, 9

T – Thanksgiving: Expression of gratitude, especially to God. 1 Samuel 2: 1 – 5, Exodus 15: 1 – 19

S – Supplication: Making a humble petition to somebody. This will also include interceding for others. 1 Samuel 1:9–13, Genesis 18:23 – 33, Exodus 32:30 -35

Every child should learn to pray in this simple way. It is the sequence that a complete prayer should take.

APPENDIX F

Excerpt from a Keynote Address presented at the second biennial women conference of the Mothers' Union and Women's Guild, Uka Ndi Igbo, New York, on Saturday 1st November 2008 By Mrs. Ngozi Martin-Oguike.

Conference Theme: Love in Christian Homes

Love is an integral part of the fruit of the Spirit (Galatians 5:22, 23), a manifestation of an inner feeling of affection and care. The Webster Dictionary defines love as any of a number of emotions and experiences related to a sense of strong affection.1 Corinthians 13 is the Bible chapter of love and utilizes the greatest and most admirable virtues in describing love with such phrases as (Verses 4 – 7): *suffers long, is kind, not envious, does not parade itself, is not puffed up, does not behave rudely, does not seek its own, is not provoked, thinks not evil, does not rejoice in iniquity but rejoices in truth, bears all things, believes all things, hopes all things and endures all things.* Verse 13 summarizes love as 'the greatest'.

Jesus defines love as the summary of the commandments. That means that the 10 commandments in Exodus 20 can be precisely expressed as **love to God and all**. Meanwhile, the family is the basic unit of the community. Family is defined by the Oxford Online Dictionary as:

1. A group consisting of two parents and their children living together as a unit.

2.   A group of people related by blood or marriage.
3.   The children of a person or couple.
4.   All the descendants of a common ancestor
5.   A group united by a significant shared characteristic

Also, Merriam Webster Dictionary defines home as:

> One's place of residence : domicile b: house 2: the social unit formed by a family living together 3 a: a familiar or usual setting : congenial environment ; also : the focus of one's domestic attention <home is where the heart is> b: habitat 4 a: a place of origin <salmon returning to their home to spawn> ; also : one's own country <having troubles at home and abroad> b: headquarters 2 <home of the dance company>5: an establishment providing residence and care for people with special needs <homes for the elderly>6: the objective in various games ; especially : home plate — at home 1: relaxed and comfortable : at ease <felt completely at home on the stage>2: in harmony with the surroundings3: on familiar ground : knowledgeable <teachers at home in their subject fields>

Therefore, home transcends family in the aspect of satisfaction and that is why the saying that 'money can buy a house but not a home.'

The Christian Home

The definition of Christian home may be enlarged to mean the household of God. A single home is the nucleus of the society. The old saying goes that 'charity begins at home', as such, if our homes do not experience charity (that is, love in practice), we should not expect a loving, wholesome society. The home is supposed to provide a safe haven for family members. A feeling of wellbeing and the absence of fear are qualities found in a good home. Members of a family live in the home, just as children of God are supposed to make up the church family.

Even secular dictionaries acknowledge the wholesomeness of the home. We join to say, 'East, west, north and south, there is no place like home'. Consequently, to have love in the family requires that there is an understanding of the key point of love, which is written in scripture: 'Beloved, let us love one another, for love is of God and anyone who loves is born of God and knows God. He that loves not, knows not God, for God is love' (I John 4:7, 8). Therefore a Christian home is expected to radiate the character of God. This love is the essence of our being and as true Christians we must live God's kind of life.

Types of love
There are at least 9 types of love, as expressed in the English language. These are: Affection, sexual love, platonic love, romantic love, puppy love, friendship, committed love, infatuation and passionate love. As Christians and for the purpose of our conference, I will limit us to 3 types of love, as used in scriptures:

Philos: The love of a child for a parent, friendship, and brotherly love. It is derived from: filial love. A person is not bound to care about someone who is not related to him or her.

Eros: This is passionate love, with sensual desire and longing. The modern Greek word "*erotas*" means romantic love. The term *erotic* is derived from *eros*. This often has a condition on which it is built and can easily fade.

Agape: This is the major word interpreted as 'love' in the New Testament. The concept of agape is not limited to God's love of humanity; it could also be used to describe the love one person has for another. In contrast to the sensuous love of *eros* or the friendship expressed by *philos*, agape describes unselfish kind of love that consists of giving without anticipation of anything in return, or deep caring love for everyone.

Paul and Agape

In St. Paul's theology, love is a result of faith in God. When we have enough faith and trust in God, the Holy Spirit gives us the gift of love as a sign of what is ahead in the Kingdom of God. Love is therefore not a product of human views or sentiments — it is not possible for mere humans to practise genuine love. Love is a fruit of the Spirit, which comes only when we let Christ live within us. That's why many non-Christians do not really know or experience real love. Their love is always with vested interest and they do nothing without ulterior motives.

Love demonstrates the importance of a sound Christian foundation, upon which families should be built. Good Christian values need to be upheld to the glory of God. The disciples of Christ should work together to establish stable homes because we cannot be addressed as Christians without any testimony. Christianity must be known for radiating the lifestyle of Christ, which comes with a lot of discipline. For instance, when you ask a person to control his alcohol intake, you are expecting him to be the master of his habits and not to make himself subjugated by his drinking habits, knowing that the effects of being ruled by carnal desires is destructive. Such a person loses the ability to be responsible for his/her own actions. Therefore, a child of God must be sober and vigilant. Self-control is part of the fruit of the Spirit just like love and they all rule in the Christian home. One does not go without the other.

Bearing fruit

The first test of true discipleship is fruit bearing. Do you bear the fruit of the Spirit or the works of the devil? (Galatians 5:19 –22). This fruit must manifest in Christian homes: 'Be sober and self-controlled. Be watchful. Your adversary, the devil, walks around like a roaring lion, seeking whom he may devour' (I Peter 5:8). A prayerful family would stand together to conquer by bearing the fruit of the Spirit.

Love in the family

Today we discuss our families as peculiar sets of people, a community of people who, like the pilgrims of old, have left our 'native' land to dwell in a land across the seas and far away and, in Biblical terms, 'unto the uttermost parts of the earth.' The common description of our situation today is Diasporas– immigrants, pilgrims, Africans, Nigerians or Igbos in Diasporas. Whatever be your title, along with your family members, you share in a new tradition, an emerging culture that is shaped by a ruthless socio-political and economic environment; a hegemony that thinks from a one-point perspective, the narrow-minded. This culture has enslaved many. It has produced a new brand of slavery that is even more dangerous than the former, a mental and spiritual slavery with debilitating effect on the family, the major support system that God Himself gave to man in Eden. This is the slavery that will wipe away our race, if we refuse to return to the basics. The erosion of family values shall crumble Africans in Diasporas and leave many in regrets, except we all rise now and face the challenge of keeping the family intact. The other option is the very thing we all dread, becoming a people without roots and traditions, becoming a prey in the land.

I sound the trumpet in the land because there is a dire need to awake from slumber and rise and shine. The classic story of *Roots* by Alex Haley and other historical stories teach us that the slaves in plantations bounced back on the love of their families and community for strength in their most trying times. But today we see that in the struggle for economic actualization husbands forsake their wives and vice versa. Therefore, many die alone, with hatred and acrimony; so where do we go from here? Stories abound of our people caught up in the rat race. The gravity of the consequences is all too disturbing.

In the pseudo-Christian dilemma that we seem to operate, many do not find time to strengthen their faith. Consequently, we are surrounded by half-baked Christians who operate like what Americans refer to as 'dummies'. But there should be no Christian dummies. The Bible says, 'If any man is in Christ he is a new creature, old things have passed away; behold all things have become new' (II Corinthians 5:17). If all things are new in the lives of Christians, we must experience a positive society. But the reverse is the case. Although so many of our people profess Christianity, they manifest an unprecedented level of worldliness that neutralizes their confession of faith.

If new creatures live together, they are sure to remain fresh and clean; but the mixture of the new and the old produces a result that is neutralized, unpalatable, pale and unhealthy. The old wine in a new wineskin, as described by Jesus in Matthew 9:17, only produces a shrunken wineskin. This leads us to the foundations of a true Christian family. 'Be not unequally yoked together with unbelievers' (II Corinthians 6:14) – Christians should marry Christians and remain in the faith. This should be our counsel to our children as they grow and make their own families. Sincere Christians uphold the faith of each other.

Our method of handling conflicts also shows the quality of our Christianity. In my study of many couples that have had serious problems in their marriages, I have identified three major causes of conflict which have topped the rest. These are: Pride, promiscuity (unfaithfulness) and pursuit of wealth (the love of money).

Pride

Pride goeth before destruction, and a haughty spirit before a fall.
(Proverbs16:18)

Most families or relationships crumble because no one is ready to concede defeat. This happens in families, as it is in politics. Pride is a killer. It is a cancer that destroys the spiritual life of anyone who gives it the chance. The person who is always right, does not obey authority, wants to be seen and heard and takes no correction is doomed to failure. That person is never content because there is always someone better than the other in a given community, so there is an endless quest for actualization, which never comes. When pride enters into a home, fault-finding follows; hence, all kinds of competition sets in, leading to haughtiness, disrespect for one another and God-given authority. Just as it was in the case of Lucifer, the favour of God is lost in such a situation. Pride has only one opposite: humility. A humble person has a meek and quiet spirit and is able to communicate with God. When people are humble, they cry in helplessness to God. They seek help, knowing that their needs can weigh them down. They are prayerful, always on their knee to conquer.

'The meek shall inherit the earth' (Matthew 5:5). It was initially hard for me to understand this verse of the beatitudes. The meek appeared to be weak, until I encountered the word in its true sense. I came to understand that meekness is so simple and uncomplicated. I found that the reverse is arrogance and selfishness. Humility stabilizes you. People prefer to relate to the meek and humble than to the proud and conceited.

In any society, the more humble a person is, the more he or she receives open doors. It is good to note that humility is not weakness or stupidity. It is not ignorance of your rights, neither is it the inability to stand firm. Humility simply brings you to the feet of Jesus, just like Mary (Luke 10:38–42) to seek the Lord's way. Praying and studying the Word of God in the home is the way to go. With humility, meekness and prayerfulness, the family is set on the path of success.

Promiscuity (unfaithfulness)

This is the result of the breaking of the marriage vow, which is as follows:

Minister to Groom: *Do you........ take........... to be your wife– to live together after God's ordinance in the holy estate of matrimony? Will you love her, comfort her, honour and keep her, in sickness and in health, for richer, for poorer, for better, for worse, in sadness and in joy, to cherish and continually bestow upon her your heart's deepest devotion, forsaking all others, keep yourself only unto her as long as you both shall live?*

Groom: *I will.*

Minister to Bride: *Do you........... take......... to be your husband – to live together after God's ordinance – in the holy estate of matrimony? Will you love him, comfort him, honour and keep him, in sickness and in health, for richer, for poorer, for better, for worse, in sadness and in joy, to cherish and continually bestow upon him your heart's deepest devotion, **forsaking all others, keep yourself only unto him as long as you both shall live?***

Bride: *I will.* (www.weddingplanninglinks.com)

The above is a sample of the traditional marriage vow. *'Forsaking all others, keep yourself only unto him/her as long as you both shall live'* seems to be the hardest part of the vow for so many couples. It is a rampant occurrence now to have couples breaking this vow. There is a lack of faithfulness. There is a love for illicit behaviour that seems to develop around us. Many seem to think that by living in another part of the world far from home, they have escaped the prowling eyes of God and can do just what they wish. They seem to be suffering from a prolonged culture shock.

Nevertheless, a married man or woman cannot afford to sacrifice his or her home at the altar of carnal pleasure. Many have compromised standards by thinking that they no longer need their family. The result is that they leave very little or no legacies for those who come behind; our priced possessions, our children. It is like the Igbo adage, 'the dog has eaten the dung, but the goat's teeth are decayed.' How can we allow our next generation to be victims of the sins of their predecessors? (Exodus 20:5).

In a nutshell, we must abstain from this most divisive sin: adultery. The reason is that it is the only sin the Bible gave as a condition for divorce: *But I tell you that anyone who **divorces** his wife, except for marital unfaithfulness, causes her to become an adulteress; and anyone who marries the **divorced** woman commits adultery* (Matthew 5:32).

Where there is lack of forgiveness and reconciliation, the end of adultery is often divorce. It is a sin that eats up the doer and makes him or her ashamed. It comes gently and subtly, but can be avoided through prayers and the study of the word of God individually and corporately.

Call for Help

At the earliest sign of promiscuous or lustful thoughts and attitudes, please ask for help and turn away completely from the attraction (Matthew 5:28). The fastest help comes through sincere prayer. Many stories we hear around us today are only good enough for Hollywood and not conducive as real life experiences. The reason is that certain experiences would only end up destroying the victims and affecting the very foundation of family life. God hates iniquity.

If you have already gone astray and sinned against God, your spouse and your body, who are we to condemn you? There are no perfect persons, but there are repentant souls, who are saved and renewed. That is the best place to be. Jesus said to the adulterous woman, 'Neither do I condemn you, go and sin no more' (John 8:11b). 'Therefore, if anyone is in Christ, he is a new creature, old things have passed away, behold all things have become new' (II Corinthians 5:17). The fountain of His blood still flows; come and receive cleansing, for 'as many as received Him, He gave power to become Children of God' (John 1:12). Therefore, my sisters and brothers, ask for help from true elders of the church and do not return to sin and iniquity. Return and follow the Lord. You will be free indeed.

The Pursuit of Wealth (the love of money)

"For the love of money is the root of all evil: which while some coveted after, they have erred from the faith, and pierced themselves through with many sorrows' (I Timothy 6:10). *'He who is greedy for gain troubles his own house"* (Proverbs 15:27). The question that the Bible asks Diasporas families who cast away caution in order to make money in this land, thereby inviting conflicts

to their homes is: 'For what shall it profit a man if he shall gain the whole world and lose his own soul; what can you give in exchange for your soul?' (Mark 8:36, 37). Money is good, but the lust after it can create so much stress around us that we soon lose sight of the value of life. This is what happens when we give priority to wealth while forgetting the giver of all things: God Himself.

In effect, many forfeit the family which is the bedrock of our wellness. We do understand that many immigrants are in this country for 'greener pastures'. The question is often: 'then why don't we pursue the money?' My response will be, do all things with moderation, because *a man's life does not consist* in the *abundance of his possessions* (Luke 12:15). There is something more enduring than material wealth: your spirit, your soul.

Recently, I was listening to a radio programme in which a 73-years old man was asking a younger woman for a relationship. The presenter of the programme helped him make calls to a number of young ladies who rejected his sweet talk and wanted nothing to do with such an old man. Finally, a 63-years old lady was invited to speak to him and she bluntly said to him, 'Any woman in her sixties who wants you at 73 needs nothing else but your money. If you aint rich, you're no good.' It appears so funny, but it is blatantly true. Money has been a driving force for many families. Check your heart!

Money is a false foundation, the idol upon which many homes are built. Building a relationship upon wealth and money is like constructing a house upon sand; of course, it would not withstand floods and winds. When wealth can no longer flow, the 'love' fades and turns into tolerance and the odds become so glaring that the centre no longer holds. Contemporary issues that have destroyed many of our people in this land hinge around marrying in expectation of exploiting the spouse for riches. When the desired wealth does not give the satisfaction that was anticipated, everything begins to go wrong. The recent tides of violence across the United States bring tears to our eyes. Sisters, wipe your tears, don't give in to self-pity. There is work to be done!

Time would fail me to comment on some of the stories of spouses who have lost their lives in the struggle to keep their family intact in a foreign land. What would we gain if we give in to strife in this country that has declared zero tolerance to domestic violence? We are not a violent people. Our forefathers were the most hardworking and ingenious people on our shores. What has befallen us in this strange land? Unfortunately, wife-beating and molestation have become the order of the day. Women are practically over-worked, many mothers lose their dignity and are exposed to nightlife and parties in a trend that leave them suspect. The result is acrimony and rancour in the home; child neglect and a decadent society.

Conclusion

Please do your best to know what is happening around you and do speak out if you are experiencing any form of violence, because most of the victims of domestic violence are women who needed help but spoke too late. My slogan is: 'Domestic violence thrives on silence. Please give a loud shout!' "Are you abused? Call a sister, call the pastor, and ask for prayers.

That's informative enough." "Don't cover and die. Speak and live." "Say No to violence. Call a friend!"

Finally, many do not keep the family altar burning, so their homes cannot be seen from the rescue station. Christian women, let's arise and build our homes on the power of the Holy Spirit. Let's be spiritually awake. Let's stop playing God and allow the King to reign supreme in our marriages. Let's raise our children with love and inculcate the love of Christ into their lives, so that they are not caught unawares.

Let us be a band of praying women who know that we can have a relationship with the Lord and overcome all hardships. You must be born again (John3:3); you must hold unto the love that caused His blood to flow on Calvary's tree. Let's pray for transformation and new life in Christ both for us and our families. Let's bring our marriages and homes to the altar of deliverance and, as we arise from this conference, become a holy people unto the Lord.

My prayer is that we shall love one another, husband and wife, sons and daughters, extended family members and all people, even as Christ loved us.

Thank you so much for listening so patiently.

Ngozi Martin-Oguike
Pastor's Wife
Mothers' Union Enrolling Member
November 1, 2008.

Check out some of these online resources:

Violence in Nigerian families – http://nigeriaworld.com.

http://marriage.families.com/blog/marriage-after-divorce

http://www.askoxford.com/concise_oed/family?view=uk

http://www.merriam-webster.com/dictionary/Home

http://www.weddingplanninglinks.com/planning

http://www.rootsthebook.com/

http://www.biblegateway.com/

http://www.marriagemax.com/stop-divorce-g.asp

http://blog.worldvillage.com/family